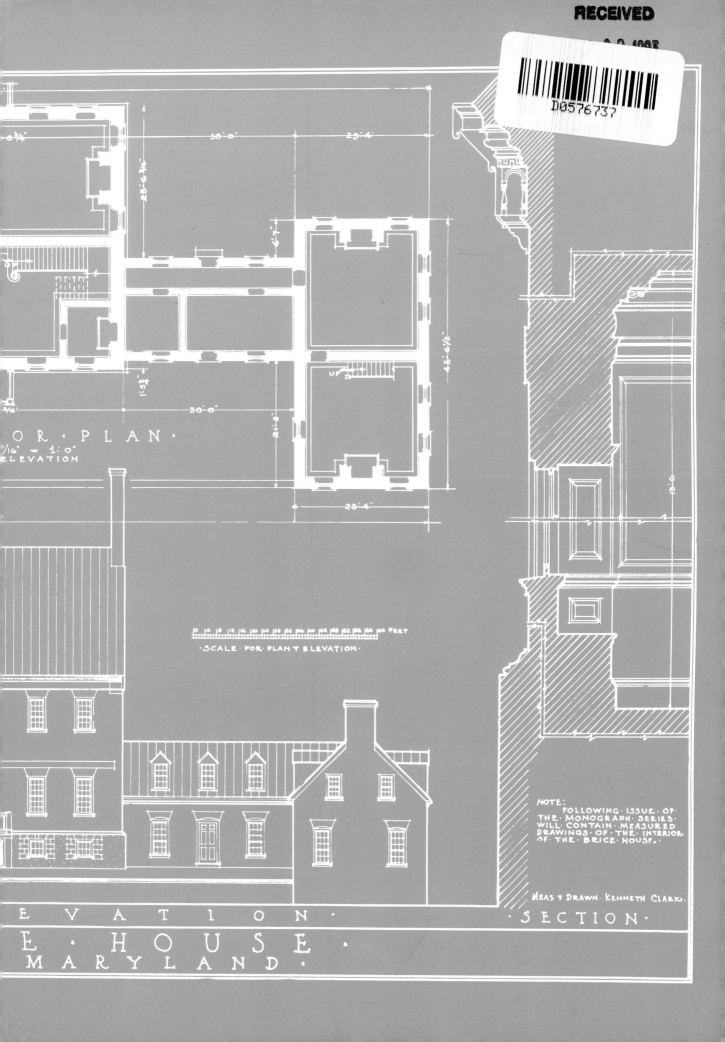

·OR·PLAN·

3/16" = 1:0"
ELEVATION

·SCALE·FOR·PLAN·T·ELEVATION·

10 14 18 112 116 120 124 128 132 136 140 144 148 152 156 160 164 FEET

NOTE:
    FOLLOWING·ISSUE·OF·
THE·MONOGRAPH·SERIES·
WILL·CONTAIN·MEASURED·
DRAWINGS·OF·THE·INTERIOR·
OF·THE·BRICE·HOUSE·

MEAS·†·DRAWN·KENNETH·CLARK·

·SECTION·

·E·V·A·T·I·O·N·

·E·H·O·U·S·E·

·M·A·R·Y·L·A·N·D·

HOMES OF NEW YORK
AND CONNECTICUT

Other National Historical Society Publications:

THE IMAGE OF WAR: 1861–1865

TOUCHED BY FIRE: A PHOTOGRAPHIC PORTRAIT OF THE CIVIL WAR

WAR OF THE REBELLION: OFFICIAL RECORDS
  OF THE UNION AND CONFEDERATE ARMIES

OFFICIAL RECORDS OF THE UNION AND CONFEDERATE NAVIES
  IN THE WAR OF THE REBELLION

HISTORICAL TIMES ILLUSTRATED ENCYCLOPEDIA OF THE CIVIL WAR

A TRAVELLER'S GUIDE TO GREAT BRITAIN SERIES

For information about National Historical Society Publications, write:
Historical Times, Inc., 2245 Kohn Road, Box 8200, Harrisburg, Pennsylvania 17105

Architectural Treasures of Early America

HOMES OF NEW YORK AND CONNECTICUT

From material originally published as
The White Pine Series of Architectural Monographs
edited by
Russell F. Whitehead and Frank Chouteau Brown

Lisa C. Mullins, Editor

Roy Underhill, Consultant

A Publication of
THE NATIONAL HISTORICAL SOCIETY

Library of Congress Cataloging-in-Publication Data

The Homes of New York and Connecticut
    (Architectural treasures of early America; 5)
    1. Architecture, Domestic—New York. 2. Architecture,
Colonial—New York. 3. Architecture, Domestic—
Connecticut. 4. Architecture, Colonial—Connecticut.
I. Mullins, Lisa C. II. Underhill, Roy. III. Series:
Architectural treasures of Early America (Harrisburg,
Pa.); 5
NA7235.N7H66   1988   728.3'7'09747   87-14215
ISBN 0-918678-24-2

The original photographs reproduced in this publication are from
the collection of drawings and photographs in "The White Pine
Monograph Series, Collected and Edited by Russell F. Whitehead,
The George P. Lindsay Collection." The collection, part of
the research and reference collections of The American Institute
of Architects, Washington, D.C., was acquired by the Institute
in 1955 from the Whitehead estate, through the cooperation of Mrs.
Russell F. Whitehead, and the generosity of the Weyerhauser
Timber Company, which purchased the collection for presentation
to the Institute. The research and reference collections of the
Institute are available for public use. A written request for such
use is required so that space may be reserved and assistance made
available.

CONTENTS

A CONNECTICUT HOUSE FRAME ON A CARIBBEAN ISLAND

London 29th Febry 1764

To Mr. Joseph Trumble

Sir

I want a Frame for a House, & Lumber to Compleat that Frame, which I fancy may be had very well from Connecticut in New England & desire you to undertake to provide the same for me, on the Lowest Terms, they are to be had for these; & ship the same to me, to the Island of Granada, in the West Indies, . . . I must also desire You to procure some Two or three Carpenters & Joiners, who shall come out, with the Frame & Lumber, to the s^d Island of Granada, to sett up & finish the same, . . . Write to me at the Granades, . . . that I may know what Time I may expect the arrival of this Vessell at the above Port — I am Sir Your most Humb^le Servt

Dr. Wm Bryant

News of the letter from London traveled fast among the workmen of East Haddam, Connecticut. Work was always welcome in the riverfront town, and the prospect of sailing to the West Indies along with the doctor's house frame made for doubled excitement. The contract was no less welcome to Joseph Trumbull and his business partners. The years following the French and Indian War had not been good for them, and the opportunity to parlay their shipbuilding experience into a timber frame exporting business could save them from bankruptcy. If this contract was successfully completed, they might receive further commissions. The tropical island had been taken from the French only two years before, and there was talk of building a hospital and other government buildings.

Joseph Trumbull wrote to his partners of the prospects for the workmen, "As for Joiners, to go to Granada . . . I think if they . . . are careful and prudent, it must be a good Jobb for them . . . it will be best for one of them at least to Work in the Frames, that he may be the Better able to sett them up." The lead carpenter hired by the Trumbull firm was Isaac Fitch of Lebanon, Connecticut. Although he and his helpers built the house frame that summer, Isaac Fitch was not the one to "go to Granada." He remained to build the New London County Court House and some of the finest homes in Connecticut.†

The pine timbers and sweat came from Connecticut, but the design was from the London doctor and his West Indian wife. Specifications, a plan and elevation for the house accompanied the letter commissioning its construction.

"The great House to be Fifty feet by twenty feet with Galleries on the front and back. The great house to be two storys high — the Posts 19 feet long, to be equally divided for the two Storys — the Posts of the Gallery's to be hewed Octogons & Plained, Seventeen feet Long."

---

†For more on the life and work of Isaac Fitch see William L. Warren, *Isaac Fitch of Lebanon, Connecticut Master Joiner* 1734–1791, Hartford, The Antiquarian & Landmarks Society, Inc., of Connecticut, 1978.

The Connecticut men may have found it an odd house frame to cut and fit, but the octagonal porch columns were easy work for men experienced in hewing shipmasts. The two-story high porches on the front and back of the house would protect it from the tropical sun. The specifications also made it clear where corners were to be cut—and where they were to be beaded. "the Ground floor Timbers to be large & Strong & . . . hewed on one Side only," but "the Posts, Studds, Beams & Joists, that come in sight of the Chambers, to be plained, & a Bead run on the Edges."

The frame was soon ready and loaded aboard the brigantine *Olive*, which sailed from New London, Connecticut, in late July. The size of the ship made it "necessary to Splice the long Sticks of Lumber as they can't be Stowed on Board the Vessell." The bill for the house was recorded as paid by mid-October of that same year. Who would believe that a house could be ordered in England, framed in Connecticut, delivered two thousand miles away in the West Indies, completed and paid for—all in the space of seven months?

But this was nothing new to these Yankee builders, or to any carpenters of the old tradition. One or two skilled craftsmen could cut the joints in the timbers for houses, bridges and windmills, and only hire the big crew for the few days required to assemble and raise the frame on the site. The first building in Windsor, Connecticut, was actually prefabricated in Plymouth, Massachusetts. In 1633 it was carried two hundred miles by sea around the Cape and then fifty miles up the Connecticut River to Windsor. Later, the flow reversed and this same town of Windsor became the source of houses. In Chapter 11 of this volume, we learn of a house on Main Street in Essex, Connecticut, with an unusual hipped roof. Apparently, there was a carpenter in Windsor "who knew the secrets of cutting rafter bevels and such, and instead of travelling about to do the work stayed comfortably at home and shipped the shaped lumber."

These days, the timber frame and transport tradition is going strong. The economic advantages of pre-fabricating the parts of a house in a shop or workyard, coupled with the aesthetic appeal of exposed timbers has spawned a renaissance of this ancient trade. The Timber Framers Guild of North America build everything from medieval to ultra-modern timber frames. So, choose the house that you like from this book and commission your builder. Your house, a stack of numbered timbers, will soon be waiting for you at the dock. The framing and finish may be a little different from that of 1764, but the excitement you share will be identical, right down to the final peg.

ROY UNDERHILL
MASTER HOUSEWRIGHT
COLONIAL WILLIAMSBURG

Rensselaerville, New York

Text by
William A. Keller
Photographs by
Kenneth Clark
Originally published in 1924 as White Pine Monograph
Volume X, Number 4

Entrance Detail
STEVENS HOUSE, RENSSELAERVILLE, NEW YORK

RENSSELAERVILLE:
AN OLD VILLAGE OF THE HELDERBERGS

AFTER climbing some fourteen hundred feet over the high rocky ledge known as The Helderbergs, in the southwestern part of Albany County, New York State, one comes upon a sequestered village—a village not perched upon a commanding hilltop, as one might expect, but half hidden in a sheltered hollow surrounded by wooded hills, and now comprising all that is left of a once thriving and populous settlement; a unique village, still twenty-eight miles away from a railroad, overlooked by the majestic Catskill Range.

"On account of the slow growth of the Colony of New Netherlands, the Dutch States were induced, in 1629, to pass an ordinance granting to any member of The West India Company the right of selecting any tract of land, outside of the Island of Manhattan, 16 miles on one side, or 8 miles on either side, of any navigable stream, and extending as far inland as the patroon, (as the proprietor was called) should choose.

The chief conditions imposed were the establishment of a colony of at least 50 persons over 15 years of age, within four years, and the payment of 5 percent on all trade except that in furs.

Under these grants, Kilean Van Rensselaer, a director in this Company, secured, with additional purchases made through his agents, land twenty-four miles each side of the Hudson, and forty-eight miles inland, constituting Rensselaerwyck, and including what is now Albany County, most of Rensselaer County, and a part of the County of Columbia."

At the close of the Revolutionary War, The Manor of Rensselaerwyck was held by Stephen Van Rensselaer, and then commenced the earliest practicable attempts to settle the more remote parts of it. The Patroon of the Colony, or Lord of the Manor, as he was afterward called, gave to each settler the free use of the land for seven years; and thereafter, if the settler chose to retain it, a perpetual lease or grant in fee, subject to the payment annually of twenty-two and a half bushels of wheat, a day's service with carriage and horses, and four fat fowls, for each lot of one hundred and sixty acres.

To this remote spot, mountainous, stony, and heavily timbered, came sturdy New Englanders— "men in pursuit of labor"—and doubtless they found plenty of it, as the only way of disposing of the forests was to fell, pile and burn the trees upon the land. Ye shades of those same trees! When firewood in the vicinity sells nowadays for ten dollars or more a cord!

The date of the settlement of the village— February 22nd, 1788—is established by a letter written by the son of Samuel Jenkins, the first settler, dated February 21st, 1850, in which he says: "It will be sixty-two years tomorrow, 12 o'clock noon, since my father's family were set off the sleighs in which they were, into a log cabin in this, then a drear wilderness; to look back it appears like a short time, but the difficulties and privations for a number of years will never be forgotten."

The spring brought a party of men looking for farms, and by their united efforts a flouring mill was raised on the banks of the Ten Mile Creek, the ox power of the neighborhood bringing the millstones from the distant village of Hudson.

From this small beginning the settlement grew until in 1832 it was one of the most thriving villages in the state, its position on the post road making it an important stopping place for coaches traveling to and from the western part of New York State. The abundance of hemlock furnished great facilities for leather making. After the roads were in condition for bringing in hides, there were tanneries in every quarter of the town.

Eventually some of these tanneries burned

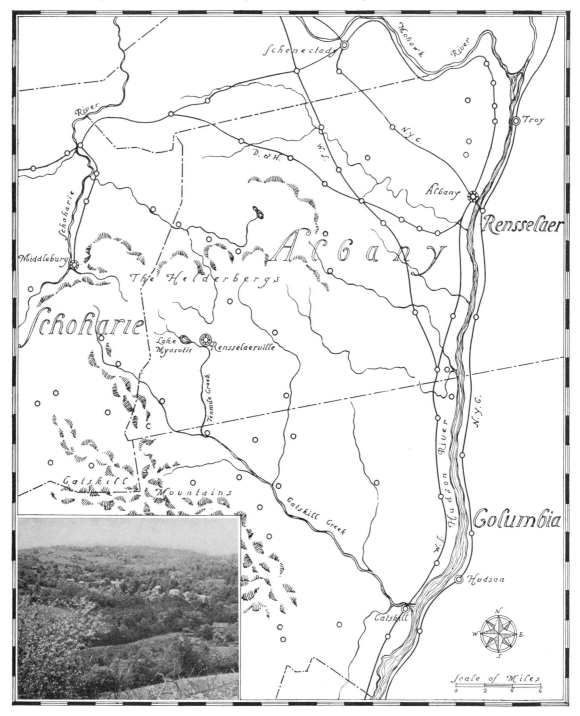

down; the supply of bark was too nearly exhausted to justify rebuilding and so, as seemed inevitable with the advent of railroads in more accessible parts of the state, the prosperity of the village gradually diminished.

The last of its activities ceased with the removal of the woolen mill which had been established there by Messrs. Huyck and Waterbury, and which was for many years one of the few woolen mills in this country.

It is through the interest of the Huyck families that the modern needs of the community have been supplied in the form of a Town Hall and a Library, and through their efforts that many of the old houses have been preserved.

Rensselaerville, as one of the early settlements in the upper Hudson region, has an interest and charm that recall to mind some of the New England villages. The forebears of some of these Rensselaerville families had originally emigrated from Connecticut, becoming pioneers in settling the east end of Long Island, especially at East Hampton, whence came a goodly quota of first settlers to Rensselaerville. Thus the influence of Connecticut architecture can be traced in some of their homes, as shown by their excellent detail and their air of primness.

While three of the houses noted in the chapter are based on the same general design, each has a distinctive interest. All have a quiet dignity due to their broad fronts, the spacing of windows balancing the enriched central motif of wide pedimented doorway, and graceful Palladian window.

The architect-builder of all but one of the Rensselaerville houses shown in the accompanying photographs was Ephraim Russ. He is mentioned in the chapters on the village history as "that estimable man and faithful builder," and indeed he did faithfully reproduce in these houses the refinement and good taste of New England architecture. That he was engaged in serving his country, as well as his townspeople, is shown by an entry in an 1812 ledger (when the Jonathan Jenkins House was being built) stating that he was advanced, in lieu of money payment, "a regimental coat, do. vest, and military hatt."

Gateway
ELDRIDGE HOUSE, RENSSELAERVILLE, NEW YORK

STEVENS HOUSE, RENSSELAERVILLE, NEW YORK
Built in 1809 by Rufus Watson.

ELDRIDGE HOUSE, RENSSELAERVILLE, NEW YORK
Built in 1806 by Daniel Conkling.

The Eldridge House, built in 1806 by Daniel Conkling, is now the summer home of Mrs. Lewis A. Eldridge, the great-granddaughter of the original owner. Standing on slightly rising ground, with the reserve naturally given by a low street wall and a white fence, the house looks out over out in this and in most of the other houses illustrated, gives one the impression of a house of greater frontage than forty-eight and one-half feet. The laminated stone of the region provided an excellent material for walls and steps. Screen doors (themselves a fly in the architectural oint-

Detail of Doorway
ELDRIDGE HOUSE, RENSSELAERVILLE, NEW YORK

the village, to the bold outline of the northern Catskills on the distant horizon. The carrying down of the plain surface of the frieze to the cornice of the Palladian window is a feature not usually found in houses of this type. The fine proportion and sash divisions, consistently carried ment!) necessitate in many of these houses a thin shelf in front of the entrance transom bar. The two-story porch at the rear is, of course, a late addition. The immense lilacs along the walk to the entrance are believed to have been set out about the time the house was built.

Rear View

JENKINS HOMESTEAD, RENSSELAERVILLE, NEW YORK

It is surprising how many taverns and other places for the entertainment of travelers were found necessary, and how large a proportion of the townsmen were endorsed by the Board of Excise as "of good moral character and sufficient intelligence to keep a public tavern." Among those

The original cornice has been restored and a box gutter formed. The original glass, most of which is still preserved, is of a pale green tone.

The Jenkins Homestead, built in 1812, has been occupied continuously by a member of the family ever since that date. There is an old

Detail of Doorway
JENKINS HOUSE, RENSSELAERVILLE, NEW YORK

"sufficiently intelligent" was one Rufus Watson, who, in 1809 built and maintained as an inn, the house now the country home of Mr. Clarence W. Stevens. No doubt its broad front, and its hospitable entrance opening almost directly upon the street, invited many a weary traveler within.

letter in which Ephraim Russ (upon being engaged to build this house) writes of his appreciation for having had a free hand in the building of the Daniel Conkling House, and rather laments that he is not to have this same opportunity with the Jenkins House.

RIDER HOUSE, RENSSELAERVILLE, NEW YORK
Built in 1823 by Eli Hutchinson.

The homestead is set back from the street among elms, maples, locusts, black walnuts, and several white pines—one patriarch pine by the roadside standing there as if to show to all passers-by its pride in the old house built of its family stock. The original sash of twenty-four lights have been replaced by those of twelve. This change is regrettably noticeable in the Palladian window, which has the old (false in this case) muntin divisions in the arched head.

The view from the rear shows not only the beautiful setting of trees, but also the great mass of the house, not appreciated by a person viewing it from the street.

In the James Rider House, built in 1823 by Eli Hutchinson, the architectural effect is accomplished by the use of plain members on a wall surface of flush siding, with the slightest projection only, for window casings. The graceful doorway, and the shallow elliptical arches, recall some of the work of central New York State. This is one of the comparatively few houses of this locality that have the gable end toward the street—an arrangement that, in later days, when lots became narrow, and domestic architecture fell to its lowest terms, made the houses on many a village street a saw-tooth row of mediocrities. Ephraim Russ, after completing this house, wrote to a friend that he had been "screwed down to the last cent." And this is by no means the only case in which the architectural result has been the better because the designer was "screwed down" to a restricted budget!

The Brock Sployd House, built in 1825 by Gurdon Conkling, is a delightful surprise to any one looking in between the quaint old gateposts, and seeing it through the half-screen of foliage. It attracts immediate attention, being so good in proportion and so "correct" in every detail. Its recessed portico of two bays, with a column in the center, is amusing. The average modern architect would say of the designer, respecting the central column, "Why did he do it?" The more—than—average architect would answer "Why shouldn't he do it?" At the left of the porch is an entry; the living room, sixteen by twenty-two feet, extends across the front, and a closet at the right balances the entry. Two gables, slightly separated, form the very unusual side elevation of this unusual house.

The Presbyterian Church, built in 1842, belongs to the Greek Revival period, and, like many others of the time, is essentially carried out along the lines of masonry architecture, though executed in wood. The effect of massive stonework is consistently obtained by the use of flush siding. One regrets the heavy steeple cornices, and that so heavy a moulding was used for the architrave.

The old buildings at the side of the church have all the fifty-seven varieties of width of siding, and

Entrance Detail

RIDER HOUSE, RENSSELAERVILLE, NEW YORK

SPLOYD HOUSE, RENSSELAERVILLE, NEW YORK
Built in 1825 by Gurdon Conkling.

Entrance Detail
SPLOYD HOUSE, RENSSELAERVILLE, NEW YORK

THE MANSE, RENSSELAERVILLE, NEW YORK
Built in 1827 by Judge John Niles.

even the siding at the ends of the Manse has a pleasing variation.

The Manse, though not immediately adjoining the Church, is only a short distance away, and was the old Judge John Niles House, built in 1827. The "rambling" of the house toward the rear only partly shows in the picture. The porch was probably the first in the village.

There is danger of the modern suburban house reverting to the porchless type of early Rensselaerville, if there is any considerable increase in the number of radio sets in use by our neighbors.

The Episcopal Church is shown in the title page sketch only, its site making it impossible to secure any good photograph. This church is another example of the work of our friend Ephraim Russ who built it in 1815. Its gallery windows, as is usually the case in these old churches, give the building the appearance of being two stories in height.

In the two churchyards "the rude forefathers of the hamlet sleep" — who, by their simple living within these Rensselaerville houses, first made them homes.

Some years ago there was published in a Rensselaerville newspaper a series of chapters on the early settlement of the village. These chapters are the only existing printed historical papers pertaining to the early settlement and they have been used as the writer's principal source of information. The author of these chapters ends her series with the hope that someone who has greater facilities for gathering information, will put it in "a form more presentable and less perishable, and for such purpose he will be quite welcome to what we have been able to contribute." Thus the heritage of her written words has come down to the writer to pass on, and in these lovely pictures especially taken for *The White Pine*

Series of Architectural Monographs is the "form more presentable and less perishable.

A word in conclusion: A just criticism of the houses of Rensselaerville might be that they look too new for buildings over one hundred years old. The answer is that they are living examples of the long life of houses built of white pine and rejuvenated with paint.

PRESBYTERIAN CHURCH—1842—RENSSELAERVILLE, NEW YORK

Cooperstown, New York:
In the Days of Our Forefathers

Text by
Frank P. Whiting
Photographs by
DeForest Coleman and Kenneth Clark
Originally published in 1923 as White Pine Monograph
Volume IX, Number 3

Detail of One of the Three Entrances
LYMAN HOUSE—1816—COLLIERSVILLE, NEAR COOPERSTOWN, NEW YORK

COOPERSTOWN:
IN THE DAYS OF OUR FOREFATHERS

THE beauty of the country surrounding Cooperstown has been immortalized in the works of James Fenimore Cooper, eleventh child of William Cooper, the founder of the town which bears his name. The dwellings of the early inhabitants were worthy of their glorious setting, but as yet their history is little known.

In a letter written some years after his first journey into this forest region of pines and hemlock and green waters, William Cooper describes his lonely venture: "In 1785 I visited the rough and hilly country of Otsego, where there existed not an inhabitant nor any trace of a road. I was alone, three hundred miles from home without food, fire and fishing tackle my only means of subsistence. My horse fed on the grass that grew by the edge of the waters. I laid me down to sleep in my watch coat, nothing but the wilderness around me. In this way I explored the country and formed my plans for future settlement and meditated upon the spot where a place of trade or a village should be established." Evidently from the chronicles written by and of William Cooper, he was a much traveled man, and was more satisfied with the beautiful country around Otsego Lake than with Pennsylvania and New Jersey, from whence he came.

There is a fascination peculiar to this region which one does not find in many places. It is

practically away from any main line railroad, midway between the Mohawk River and a valley traversed by the Delaware and Hudson Railroad. For this reason, it has kept to a great degree the old-fashioned spirit both in its manners and customs and in its architecture.

The questions suggest themselves at once how, in a country so far (at that time) from the general lines of travel, such well-designed houses were erected and to whom should be attributed their originality. The only record that I can find is of one Hooker, to whom is attributed Hyde Hall at the head of the lake. Possibly the following quotation may shed light on the matter: "During the summer of 1787 many settlers arrived, a good part of them from Connecticut and most of the land on the patent was taken up. Several small log tenements were constructed on the site of the village, and the permanent residents numbered about twenty souls. Meantime, Cooper had been extending his holdings in adjacent patents until he had most of the neighboring country under his control. Toward the end of his life, he had settled more acres than any man in America. It is more than probable that among the settlers from Connecticut and the southern part of New York there were new craftsmen who brought some knowledge of design and building which, if they had no opportunity of showing during their generation, was certainly embued into their descendants."

One may assume that the influence of William

Quotations throughout are from "The Story of Cooperstown" by the late Ralph Birdsell, formerly Rector of Christ Church. The author is indebted to this book for much of his information.

Cooper and James Fenimore Cooper was shown as the guiding hand to these craftsmen and their descendants in the design and planning of their houses. I judge this from the beautiful design of Otsego Hall, which is said to have been designed and built by William Cooper in 1799. No doubt these men, whose tastes were of the finer kind, took as much pride in the appearance of their homes as they did in the polish and finesse of their writings. Otsego Hall, (judging from the model now in the village library), was a very pretentious home for those times, and in fact might far surpass many present day houses of the same size. Its dignity of exterior and the proportions of the rooms and halls cannot be criticized.

This region, at the time of the building of many of the early houses, abounded in the finest growth of virgin pines, growing to great heights and of ample diameters for all building purposes. This, together with a native stone which quarries lik elongated brick, and other quarries at the head of the lake, where hard limestone was plentiful, must have thrilled even the humblest craftsman in his line to make and fashion from these wonderful native materials, mouldings and forms and combinations which grew more pretentious and refined as house succeeded house. Note that in all the illustrations shown, there is not one design identical with another. Many have the same outline and slope of roof, but are varied so that each has individuality.

In 1769 Richard Smith from Burlington, New Jersey, traveled up the Hudson to Albany, thence along the Mohawk Trail to Canajoharie, thence to Cooperstown. His journal, also, contains many interesting incidents relative to Otsego County: "24th: Rained again. The elevated hills of this country seem to intercept the flying vapors and draw down more moisture than more humble places . . . With three carpenters felled a white pine tree and began a canoe . . . Some trout were caught this morning 22 inches long . . . And I approached near to one rabbit whose face appeared to be of a blac color. 25th: We finished and launched our canoe into the lake. She is 32′ 7″ in length and 2′ 4″ broad."

The carpenters in those days doubtless were more than willing workers, for, judging from the

journal, from the 24th to the 25th they finished a canoe thirty-two feet long. However, strange as this may seem, the easy working of this soft wood might make such a thing possible. I have seen the most clear-grained planks, soft and of a color like rich cream, some twenty-four inches wide and three to four inches thick, come from some of the local sawmills. Through the thoughtfulness of the Clark family, who now own a majority of the woodlands surrounding the lake, the cutting of these and other trees has been stopped, so that a great deal of the virgin woodland remains.

The homes and houses of a village or community show more than all else the character of the inhabitants and they remain unspoken histories of their builders, for in those times men built their own houses under a guiding craftsman. Without some interesting incident or history connected with each, its individuality is lost, and it becomes simply a goodlooking house.

In 1769 Clinton's army camped near the Susquehanna River, at its source, and it was here that the Clinton Dam was built which was to hold back the waters of Otsego Lake until they should be released to allow the boats containing the troops and supplies to be carried some number of miles down the river. Upon the encampment site was built in 1790 what is now the oldest house still standing in Cooperstown. It was built by one Benjamin Griffen. The porch, with its Victorian detail, was probably added later. This house is in perfect repair, very livable and of charming proportions.

The old Otsego County Bank, built in 1831 and now known as the Clark Estate Office, occupies a position adjacent to the site of the Grogan hut, one of the first dwellings erected when Cooperstown was a straggling settlement. The Greek portico, with its beautiful two-storied columns, entablature and pediment, is of white pine, in perfect proportion and excellent detail.

At Oaksville, a hamlet of two or three houses and a country store, about four miles from Cooperstown, we find a house where the Classic order has been used, probably inspired by the Otsego County Bank. Its builder must have been a well-to-do farmer and a man of considerable good taste. The walls are of stone in variegated colors of beautiful hues, laid at random with

GRIFFEN HOUSE — 1790 — COOPERSTOWN, NEW YORK
The oldest house in Cooperstown, now standing.

wide white joints. Except for the blinds and casings, none of the woodwork has ever been painted, a practice characteristic of the Cooperstown region. The pediment and columns are without embellishment, deriving their undoubted beauty from exquisite proportions and from the soft

OLD OTSEGO COUNTY BANK — 1831 — COOPERSTOWN, NEW YORK
Now known as the Clark Estate Office

weathered color of aged white pine so evident even in the illustration. Altogether, this is a most interesting and unusual old house. Besides its architectural charm, it has a melancholy beauty that carries a hint of tales of ghosts and of witchcraft.

Interesting, not only architecturally, but also historically, is Fenimore, the one-time home

slender columns of the main façade, the simple pediment and the old-fashioned downstairs kitchen, however, are typical of the houses of the comfortably-off farmers of the region and period.

Quoting an interesting incident that occurred shortly after Cooper lived at Fenimore: "While alterations were in progress at Otsego Hall, Cooper had as his guest Samuel F. B. Morse,

HOUSE AT OAKSVILLE, FOUR MILES FROM COOPERSTOWN, NEW YORK

of James Fenimore Cooper, famous chronicler of Mohican legends and lore. It is not in Cooperstown proper, but on the shore of Otsego Lake, and is still in the possession of the present James Fenimore Cooper. Sometime after his marriage, the writer moved into Otsego Hall, in the village. Fenimore has undergone a change that is detrimental to its otherwise quaint and pleasing character—the porch overlooking the lake is a later and not too well considered addition. The

who assisted him in carrying out his orders for the reconstruction of the hall and drew designs which gave it more the style of an English country house. The local gossips said that Morse aspired to the hand of his friend's eldest daughter. Cooper had no mind to yield so fair a prize to an impecunious painter, a widower and almost forty-three; Morse was at this time experimenting with the telegraph instrument which was afterward to bring him wealth and fame as an inventor

PRESTON HOUSE, COLLIERSVILLE, NEW YORK
Built by Col. Alfred Mumford in 1827.

and to overshadow his reputation as an artist."

The Worthington Homestead, on Main Street, built in 1802, was known at that time as The White House. It differs greatly in style from any of its neighboring contemporaries. Interest in Greek forms as precedents for American domestic architecture was at its height in 1830 — this house had embodied the best forms of the Revival a quarter of a century earlier than did many houses built elsewhere and for this reason The White House of Cooperstown is unique.

"A country house of classic poise and sym-

FENIMORE, NEAR COOPERSTOWN, NEW YORK
One-time Residence of James Fenimore Cooper.

FENIMORE, COOPERSTOWN, NEW YORK
Residence of James Fenimore Cooper.

HYDE HALL, ON OTSEGO LAKE, SEVEN MILES FROM COOPERSTOWN

TIN TOP, GATE LODGE OF HYDE HALL

HYDE HALL, AT THE HEAD OF OTSEGO LAKE, SEVEN MILES FROM COOPERSTOWN

metry was designed in 1829 when Eben B. More-house purchased a few acres from the Bowers estate, on the side of Mt. Vision, at the point where the old state road made its first turn to ascend the mountain, and there erected the dwelling called Woodside Hall. For many years an Indian wigwam stood on the site now occupied by Woodside. This old stone house, set on

lost in the grounds of Woodside. It was in 1839 when Judge Morehouse gave a large evening reception for President Martin Van Buren. After the reception, when the guests had departed, Mr. Van Buren and a friend who accompanied him became separated from their companions, and lost their way in attempting to find the gate tower. For a long time they wandered and groped

THE WHITE HOUSE (WORTHINGTON HOMESTEAD)—1802—MAIN STREET, COOPERSTOWN

the hillside against a background of dense pine forest, has an air of singular dignity and repose. Standing at the head of the ascending road which continues the main street of the village, Woodside, with its row of columns gleaming white amid the living green of the forest, may be seen from almost any point along the main thoroughfare of Cooperstown.

"A President of the United States was once

about in the darkness of the grounds, finally returning to the house for a guide and a lantern, just as the family were going to bed."

The columns and entablature of Woodside are beautiful in detail and execution and are probably the most perfect in scale of any in Cooperstown. The columns are reeded and terminate in graceful Ionic capitals. Reeded columns seem to have been used frequently in this local-

ROBERT CAMPBELL HOUSE—1807—LAKE STREET, COOPERSTOWN, NEW YORK

WOODSIDE HALL—1829—COOPERSTOWN, NEW YORK

PRESTON HOUSE — 1827 — COLLIERSVILLE, NEW YORK

ity, a treatment quite as effective as fluting. The doorway is of later design, and, as seems to be true of all later additions to these stately houses, is not as interesting as the rest of the house.

Taken as a whole, Woodside is a particularly happy example of what can be achieved from a well designed combination of wood and stone. Seven miles from Cooperstown at the head of

LYMAN HOUSE — 1816 — COLLIERSVILLE, NEAR COOPERSTOWN, NEW YORK

Otsego Lake, and half a mile from both the east and the west roads around the lake, is Hyde Hall. In all America there is no more unique country-seat. The estate is entered through a gate house, called Tin Top because of its gilded tin dome surmounting the arched opening which connects two small, charming cottages. Some distance beyond, at the foot of a wooded hill, "The Sleeping Lion," is the house. The original house was completed by native workmen in 1815. Seventeen years later it was enlarged and a huge hall, with a dining room on one side and a drawing room on the other, was added. The workmen undoubtedly lived in or near the house while it was building, as all the work, from quarrying the stone to cutting and sawing the logs for doors and windows, must have been done on the premises.

The spirit of the true English manor house pervades the entire place, and is maintained in the interior. The main hall as I remember is paved with stone and there ascends from it a circular staircase of solid mahogany. The woodwork throughout the adjoining rooms is also of mahogany, and over the stately mantels are portraits in oil. The long halls and alcoves, the paved courtyards and the old-time kitchens, with cranes and spits, are in perfect keeping. Much might be said of this grand house, and many interesting stories told in connection with it if space would permit.

George Clark, the builder of Hyde Hall, was the grandson of George Clark, colonial governor of New York from 1737 to 1744, and inherited a portion of his grandfather's vast estate in Cooperstown.

"When Ambrose Jordan began the practice of law in Cooperstown, he planted an elm tree on Chestnut Street, in front of his house, at the northwest corner of Main Street. This elm, grown to mighty proportions, celebrated its one hundredth birthday in 1913. Within a few paces of the corner, facing on Main Street, and in the rear of the dwelling which fronts Chestnut Street, stands the small building that Jordan occupied as an office. This is one of the few remaining examples of the detached law offices which were common in Cooperstown, as in other villages, in early days, and often stood in the dooryard of a lawyer's residence, apart from the dwelling."

Robert Campbell, of the well-known Cherry Valley family, built for his residence, in 1807, the house that still stands on Lake Street; one façade, overlooking an old-fashioned garden, commands a beautiful view of the lake. The proportions of the house are pleasing; its cornice is ornamented by a row of triglyphs, exceptionally refined in detail. This treatment is also repeated over the windows.

All these dwellings which were built in Cooperstown in the late eighteenth and early nineteenth centuries remain today to perpetuate the spirit of the region. As a rule, the old wood-built houses have outlived the stone ones. This may be attributed to the fact that the lime mortar has given way where exposed to frost and rain.

In conclusion, let me say that if the introduction of the mansard roof and ugly brick fronts with arched windows had never pervaded Cooperstown, we would still have a village where both the commercial buildings and private dwellings were in perfect harmony.

OTSEGO LAKE FROM COOPERSTOWN, NEW YORK

Middle Doorway

End Doorway

LYMAN HOUSE, COLLIERSVILLE, NEAR COOPERSTOWN, NEW YORK

Some Forgotten Farmhouses
on Manhattan Island

Text by
Lemuel Hoadley Fowler
Photographs by
Kenneth Clark
Originally published in 1923 as White Pine Monograph
Volume IX, Number 1

ROGER MORRIS OR JUMEL MANSION, NEW YORK, NEW YORK

Built by Roger Morris in 1765. The house was bought by Stephen Jumel in 1810 and was then restored, not however as tradition has it, to the condition in Washington's time, but in the way most fashionable in his own day.

SOME FORGOTTEN FARMHOUSES
ON MANHATTAN ISLAND

EARLY "stranger's in America," those gentle-men who, in former years, came on flying trips and wrote long and uncomplimentary books about the citizens of these more or less United States, made many remarkable discoveries about us. All early travelers without exception noted with a disapproving eye the American country house. Even in recent years one stately and dig-nified English scholar said while lecturing here, "Your wooden houses, I can't understand. Why don't you put up something in stone and brick that will be solid at the end of three hundred years, as we do in England?" An American to whom the query was put, answered "It is because we don't want that kind of a house. Changes, improvements, new comforts of all sorts come so fast that we don't want a house to last too long. This house is what I want, but not what my children will want. Even I want to make some structural changes every ten years. I can now do it without being ruined, as I could not do in one of your three-century dwellings." "Bless my heart," replied the visitor, "I never thought of that. You want houses that will easily take on improvements as they come, and be free to build a new and better one every generation, if you want to."

While this explanation of the use of wood in building is, to a certain extent, ingenuous, it is,

to say the least, misleading. It does, however, suggest a reason for the small number of Colonial houses of outstanding importance that are still in existence in Greater New York. Each suc-ceeding generation took little interest in the parental home of previous times, and the place more often than not fell into strange hands; was altered, changed, and finally was torn down to make room for some newer manifestation of architectural ingenuity.

There is not, I suppose, a man alive today, who remembers the New York that was, as Henry James said, a "small but promising capital which clustered about the Battery and over-looked the Bay, and of which the uppermost boundary was indicated by the grassy wayside of Canal Street."

At the beginning of the nineteenth century there were on Manhattan Island, not one enor-mous city, but ten or more comparatively small settlements; each, in all respects, an individual, independent town. The "capital" at the lower end of the island was of course, the most impor-tant; but many conditions helped the growth of the other places from time to time. The yellow fever epidemic of 1822, for instance, did more for the fame and for an enlarged population of Greenwich Village—which, even in 1720 had been a town of considerable size—than have even the "villagers" of the present day. At the time of Lafayette's visit to the United States, one citizen informed the visitor at a reception that "I live on Varick Street, in the aristrocratic ninth ward, where all our best families dwell."

Prominent among other settlements were the Bowery Village, Corlaers Hook, Chelsea, Murray Hill, Bloomingdale; and still further north were Manhattanville, Kips Bay, New Harlem, Kingsbridge and others. Each was a town of fair size and each reproduced the essential features of the

Winkle-wise, he would have found sad havoc and confusion. Enormous, ugly brownstone flats were rearing their galvanized cornices in the air on every hand. The few scattered farm lots that remained seemed waiting in a sullen kind of way for the time when they too should be absorbed in the mad rush of flimsy, unsanitary jerry-building.

My recollections of the upper end of Manhattan Island in the 1880's are of a place that was neither city, suburb, or country. There were old

POE COTTAGE, KINGSBRIDGE ROAD, BRONX, NEW YORK, NEW YORK

Described during the poet's occupancy as — "so neat, so poor, so unfurnished and yet so charming a dwelling I never saw."

typical villages of New England. Each had its outlying farms, long tree-lined main street or its village green, its stores, church or churches, its village doctor, blacksmith, etc.

I suppose, in most cases, if one of the original settlers had wandered back to any of these places sixty years ago, that settler would have found it but little changed; possibly a little larger, but in other respects the same. In my own time, however, in the 1880's, when I first began to hunt out what was left of the houses of old New York, if that old citizen had returned Rip Van

houses to be found, tumbling down from neglect, like the Apthorp Mansion, but still, like that place, showing in spite of all neglect, some faint suggestion of their former fine style. Just when the Apthorp House was torn down I do not remember, but the loss of it was a serious one to the historian of American architecture.

You probably remember what Dr. Johnson said about woman preachers — "I told him" said Boswell, "that I had been that morning at a meeting of the people called Quakers, where I had heard a woman preach. Johnson said: 'Sir, a woman's

ROGER MORRIS OR JUMEL MANSION — 1765 — NEW YORK, NEW YORK

This general view shows the original boarding on the front of the house and the corner quoins. The east side is shingled.

preaching is like a dog walking on his hind legs—it is not done well, but you are surprised to find it done at all.'"

The same thing—but necessarily with some slight changes, it is true, might be said of these few old farmhouses on Manhattan Island. Some of them are not given proper care and their preservation has been awkwardly managed, but you are surprised to find them on Manhattan Island at all.

When they were new, and for many years after, these old places were owned by the farmers whose acres stretched out between the two rivers, on both sides of the single highway leading into the "Cittie of Nu Iarck," and the larger ones were the residences of wealthy New Yorkers of that day, who built their "country seats" in the open and undeveloped regions which, at the beginning of the nineteenth century were far from the roaring city that lay between the Bowling green and the new (John McComb's and Joseph Mangin's) City Hall.

Wood, naturally enough, has played an important part in the architectural development of American building, Except during the first years of Dutch predominence, most houses in New York were frame. And even during the days when that influence was still strong, one visitor (Peter Kalm) in 1648 wrote, "The roofs are commonly covered with tiles or shingles; the latter of which are made of the white fir tree, or *Pinus Strobus*, which grows higher up in the country. . . ." etc. The first Trinity church was frame, and going to the other possible extreme of use, so was the first theater in New York. And so, too, was the later Chappel Street theater, a frame building painted—so tradition says—an unbelievably bright red.

Practically all the farmhouses that are to be seen in the city of New York today are of distinct importance as examples of the planning and design of the best types of building erected during widely different periods in the development of Colonial and early Republican architecture.

Two extremely important frame houses are Alexander Hamilton's Grange and

Detail of Doorway
ROGER MORRIS OR JUMEL MANSION, NEW YORK, NEW YORK
A side door, put in place during the restoration work by Jumel in 1810

the Gracie House. Allan McLean Hamilton in his *Life of Alexander Hamilton* states (page 338) that the Grange was "designed by John McComb, one of the leading architects of the time."

No authority is given by the author for this statement, and he adds the rather disconcerting news, to McComb enthusiasts, that "McComb's excellent work which remains today is the old City Hall which shows the artistic *influence of Sir Christopher Wren*," (the italics do not appear on the original, they are my own) and he adds a note, more unaccountable still, to say that "The design was that of Major L'Enfant." This very definite lack of understanding of the entire situation shown by the author of the *Life* and evidenced by his confusion of two buildings of entirely dissimilar design, neither of which can be said, even remotely, to show the "influence of Wren," and far distant in their date of erection; would seem to be sufficient ground for questioning his statement of the authorship of the design.

Fiske Kimball in discussing the Grange in his recent (and remarkably satisfying) *American Domestic Architecture of the American Colonies and the Early Republic,* apparently accepts McComb's connection as designer of this house on the evidence of the *Life*. He may, also, have seen in the McComb collection in the New York Historical Society, a plan marked "Hamilton's Country Seat" which I have an indistinct recollection of having seen among the McComb papers. Mr. Kimball adds, also, "that the square headed doorway with sidelights, and usually a transom, made their ap-

pearance; first, perhaps, in McComb's house for Alexander Hamilton, the Grange, in 1801."

Judging simply from the design, without any documentary evidence, many facts such as the general form of the plan and many of the details give sufficient reason for supposing this house to have been the work of the architect of the New York City Hall.

I use the word "architect" here only after careful consideration, and in the strictest eighteenth and early nineteenth century meaning of the word—that of *"one who builds"* or who

Detail of Doorway
ROGER MORRIS OR JUMEL MANSION, NEW YORK
One of the original side doors, the only original exterior door in the house dating from 1765

DYCKMAN HOUSE—1787—BROADWAY, CORNER OF 204TH STREET, NEW YORK, NEW YORK

One of four typical New York farmhouses recently and most skillfully restored.

PRINCE HOUSE, NEAR BRIDGE STREET, FLUSHING, NEW YORK, NEW YORK
The pediment and the railed walk give distinction to the façade

"superintends the construction of a building."
It was undoubtedly in that sense, without reference to McComb as having created the design, that the word was used on the cornerstone of the City Hall. The question of the respective merits of the claims for Joseph Mangin and John McComb as designers of the City Hall are discussed at length by I. N. Phelps Stokes in his monumental work on New York, *The Iconography of Manhattan Island*.

The Gracie House, in Carl Schurz Park is an extremely fine one in its details, general proportion and design. It is now owned by the city, and is practically in original condition and needs nothing but proper repair and furnishing to make it one of the most popular museum-landmarks of the city.

Archibold Gracie, the builder, was, in his day, one of the most eminent New York merchants, and his house may be considered as an example of the best type of fine country houses of its period. It is just such a fine square building as we would imagine our forefathers to have occupied in the "glorious sea masters days," and like all early New York houses, the location upon which it stands is excellent.

Further uptown, near the northern end of the Island, is the Morris House, which was built, in 1765, by Roger Morris. This gentleman, a colonel in the British army and a staunch Loyalist, found it convenient at the outbreak of the Revolution to remove himself to other parts of the American continent. Washington occupied the estate in 1776.

Various rapid changes followed until the house eventually came into the possession of Stephen Jumel, who modernized the building in many particulars, according to early nineteenth century standards of modernization, and left it practically as it now stands. A few years ago the building was purchased by the city and is now a museum.

Of all the houses illustrated in this chapter on Manhattan's farmhouses this, perhaps shows most evidence of carefully studied architectural design and suggests on the part of the unknown designer, a definite understanding of the proper handling of the means toward a definite end in

EARLY NINETEENTH CENTURY FARMHOUSE, ELMHURST, NEW YORK, NEW YORK
The pediment, semicircular window, etc., are typical of the first years of the last century.

GAMBREL ROOF HOUSE, FLUSHING, NEW YORK, NEW YORK
The house dates probably from about 1820.

the solution of the architectural problems involved.

The porch columns running through two stories are important documents in the history of colonial architecture. Prof. Fiske Kimball, in his articles on "The Study of Colonial Architecture" in *The Architectural Review* in 1918 calls attention to the fact that "no domestic example of the free-standing colossal order has yet been proved to be of pre-Revolutionary date." If the columns that form the Jumel portico are part of the original building — and there is every indication that they are part of the intention of the original designer — the building is, as far as is known, an almost unique instance of the two story column in American domestic architecture dating from the historically accurate Colonial period.

Rawson W. Haddon in an article on this house, printed in the *Architectural Record* in July and August, 1917, has determined that the house was undoubtedly completed between May and October, 1765. As "a portico supported by pillars, embellished and finished in character" is included

in a description of the house in 1791 and as no important changes had been made in the structure between this date and the time that the Morris family left the house, there is every reason to assume the present porch to be a part of the house as it was built.*

In discussing the design of this house Mr. Haddon makes a suggestion of no great direct importance in connection with the Morris House, but of distinct interest as an addition to our knowledge of the small details of early history, that "as to design, there would have been no excuse for haphazard method in laying out the building, for architects, if not numerous, were at least not unfamiliar persons in the city. Indeed, in the year of Colonel Morris's marriage, one Theophilus Hardonbrook, who has some excellent designs to his credit, was practicing in the city as "Architect" and in looking for a possible designer for the Morris House it is not stretching the point too far to suggest one or the other

*More recently, in his *American Domestic Architecture*, Kimball states that the Morris House is the only known example of the pre-Colonial two-story free-standing column.

of the two gentlemen who announced themselves as architects in the local papers just a month before Morris probably bought the property upon which the house now stands. In the New York *Mercury*, on April 8, 1765, "DOBIE and CLOW, Builders, In Division Street, TAKE this Method of informing the Public, that they undertake to build . . . , after the London Taste. Any Gentlemen who please to employ

William Dyckman's house at 204th Street and Broadway stands on the site of a farmhouse built by his grandfather in 1666 and which was burned during the Revolution. The present house was erected in 1783. If the loss of the earlier building deprives us of a good example of the type of house occupied by the average farmer during the late seventeenth century, it is altogether probable that in its general plan the present

OLD HOUSE AT THE BRIDGE, ELMHURST, NEW YORK, NEW YORK

The house closely approximates the state of neglect that was typical of many New York farmhouses forty years ago.

them, may depend upon having their Work so done, as to bear the nicest Scrutiny. If required they will also give in Plans and Elevations, with Estimates of the Whole, in Squares, Rods and Yards, together with the Quantity of Materials Buildings of any Dimensions will take, in such a Manner as any Gentleman may know his certain cost before he begins to build." While there is no reason to suppose any connection between Dobie and Clow and the Morris House, the employment of an English architect or builder would explain these columns.

building is not entirely unlike the earlier one.

The detail, however, and the appearance of the gambrel roof, and the design of the interior finish show us in all particulars what was usual during the last years of the eighteenth century. This house, still in possession of the Dyckman family, has been restored, furnished with much of the furniture used in the building when it was new, and opened to the public as a museum. The obligation thus bestowed upon the general house building public is a great one. The good that should result from this opportunity of studying an early house properly restored and furnished should dispel much of the confusion about architectural and decorative periods in America, which quite naturally, results from the usual ignorant policy in so-called colonial museums of filling rooms with a heterogeneous mass of furnishings covering a period of almost two hundred years and allowing it to be known indiscriminately as "colonial."

few years the restoration of the house has been carried on with great care and is now well on its way toward completion.

In more distant parts of Greater New York the proportion of old houses that have escaped destruction is naturally much greater than in those parts nearer the centers of activity. In Flushing, for instance, among many others, there is the Prince House. The house has so many points of

TOM PAINE COTTAGE, NEAR THE NEW YORK CITY BOUNDARY

Old country houses and old farmhouses on Manhattan Island are disappearing, and disappearing rapidly, it is true. But many are still to be found in more distant parts of the city. In the Bronx there are many interesting old houses, though none, perhaps, can boast the interest that naturally attaches itself to the tiny Poe Cottage, where the poet lived during the years 1846 to 1849 and where he wrote "Annabel Lee", "Ulaluame" and "Eureka." The little house today looks more nearly as it did in the Poe days than at any time since he left it. During the last

interest, both in plan and design that a carefully measured set of drawings of it would be of distinct interest to the architectural profession.

In Elmhurst, you can find a farmhouse or two if you want to live a farmer's life and still be within the limits of Greater New York.

Daniel Denton wrote of them as early as 1670: "Though their low-roofed houses may seem to shut their doors against pride and luxury, yet how do they stand wide open to let charity in and out, either to assist each other, or to relieve a stranger."

ROGER MORRIS OR JUMEL MANSION, NEW YORK, NEW YORK
This beautifully designed doorway is part of the work added during the "restorations" of 1810.

Settlements on the Eastern End of Long Island

Text by
William Edgar Moran
Photographs by
Kenneth Clark
Originally published in 1919 as White Pine Monograph
Volume V, Number 2

Detail of Doorway
WEBB HOUSE — c1790 — EAST MARION, LONG ISLAND

SETTLEMENTS ON THE EASTERN END OF LONG ISLAND

L ONG Island, first outlined by Adrien Block in 1614, stretches out like a long finger between the Sound and the Ocean. Throughout its length it is practically level, except for a small area of rolling hills on the Sound side. The Island is peculiar in that, whereas the north and south sides are fertile, the center is an almost barren waste covered with scrub oak; only here and there is the land under cultivation.

The settlement of Long Island was divided between the Dutch and the English. The Dutch came from Manhattan and made their first settlements in 1635. The first deed on record is from Governor Wouter van Twiller, and is dated 1636. The English came from Connecticut and the New Haven colonies and planted their settlements on the eastern end of the Island.

The first English settlement was at Southold in September, 1640; then came Southampton in 1641; and Easthampton, then called Maidstone, in 1649. The colonists soon spread out from these centers and in a short while there was a line of little villages, much as they exist today, along the coast and the shores of Peconic Bay and Great South Bay. It is interesting to note that the English settlements, for protection from the Dutch, joined themselves to Connecticut — Southold in 1648 and Easthampton in 1657. It was not until 1664 that the Island was amalgamated with New York.

The architecture of the western end has been covered in Volume IV, Chapter 1, and will not be touched upon in this chapter. Nor will that of the north side, which will be reserved for a later chapter.

The earliest houses of which any trace remains today are usually of the pitched roof, shingle-sided type, with their various lean-tos and wings, as exemplified by the Mulford and Payne houses at Easthampton and the Mackay House at Southampton, the first dating from around 1660 and the latter from 1700.

The plan of most of the examples is of the straightforward central hall type, with rooms right and left, though there are numerous houses with a side hall, as the front of the house was often devoted to the "best parlor."

Building was almost entirely of wood, with brick chimneys, as stone in most parts of the Island is notably lacking, and the architectural design is correspondingly simple and direct. In almost every example it will be found that the cornice and main entrance comprise the entire architectural embellishment, though now and then a naïve assemblage of roofs, lean-tos and wings lends some semblance of formality to the design. In the neo-classic examples, pilasters, either on the corners, taking the place of the serviceable corner-board, or even distributed across the front, give a greater feeling of architecture to the building, despite the simplicity of the fenestration. The buildings are usually painted white, even the chimneys receiving their

HOUSE AT ORIENT, LONG ISLAND

MULFORD HOUSE — c1660 — EASTHAMPTON, LONG ISLAND

coats, a feature that might well be copied on all white houses. The chimney-caps are, either by nature or by art, all provided with black tops.

The materials, as a rule, were oak for framing and white pine for exterior finish. The construction methods are similar to those in vogue in Connecticut during the same period: oak corner posts and intermediates, sheathed or stripped and covered with hand split shingles, put on with home forged nails. In some cases the fronts were shingles and the gables siding.

The unstudied relation of openings to wall-surface and story heights of most of these

Osborne House, was built about 1802. It possesses unusual detail in cornice, entrance and second story window trim. It is one of the side-entrance plan houses. The Mott House, formerly the Osborne, also at Bellport, retains the original central feature, and, although additions have been made from time to time which have injured the design as a whole, it retains exceptionally interesting detail in porch and railing.

Southampton, one of the earliest settlements, has retained unchanged but few of its old houses; the Mackay House, 1700, being about the

ROE HOUSE, PATCHOGUE, LONG ISLAND

simple houses seems to make them perfect examples of wooden design. The great simplicity which is their main feature, combined with a naïveté in design, adds to their charm. In no case do we find very grand houses, even the neo-classic examples being human in scale, and it is their utilization as "partis" which is the chief architectural characteristic, giving value to these houses in a work of this kind.

The three little houses on Main Street in Patchogue, the Roe, the Burt and the Robinson houses, are all very much alike in design, the example here shown, the Roe House, having the most interesting doorway, and each having a pleasing side porch covering the extension.

The Livingstone Farm, at Bellport, now the

oldest. Between Southampton and Watermill is the White House, built in 1849, which shows a development in design and detail of a most interesting character.

Watermill, settled in 1642, has two very good examples, one painted and the other unpainted, both built about 1800. The Thomas Halsey House would be a well-nigh perfect example of the farmhouse, were it not for the bay; and the Anna Halsey House, which until quite recently was so surrounded by man-high box as to be almost hidden, has an interesting and very unusual door treatment.

An engaging feature of this country is the presence of windmills, examples of which may be found from Southampton to Easthampton,

HOUSE AT CUTCHOGUE, LONG ISLAND

HOUSE AT EAST MARION, LONG ISLAND

HOUSE NEAR PATCHOGUE, LONG ISLAND

HOUSE AT LAUREL, LONG ISLAND

ANNA HALSEY HOUSE — c1800 — WATERMILL, LONG ISLAND

JOHN HOWARD PAYNE HOUSE — c1660 — EASTHAMPTON, LONG ISLAND

and which are of a similar type of construction to the houses, though entirely utilitarian in character.

A perfect quarry of post-colonial remains is to be found on the narrow strip of land lying between the Sound and Peconic Bay, forming the towns of East Marion and Orient, originally Oysterponds. This country was settled in 1649, and the old records tell of houses built in the seventeenth and eighteenth centuries, but no traces of these houses remain today to identify them, unless, perhaps, they have been transformed into barns. The supposition is that, with the exception of the Webb House, they have all disappeared. The remaining houses are mostly of the story and a half type, with side or central

Detail of Doorway

HOUSE AT EAST MARION, LONG ISLAND

Detail of Cornice

HOUSE AT EAST MARION, LONG ISLAND

entrances, and they are so simple that one wonders at the care that must have been spent over the front doors. One little house, here shown, has a perfect miracle of a cornice, delicately fluted, with symmetrically spaced fluted bands, simulating triglyphs, and a cornice termination as unusual as it is ingenious. The Webb House, about 1790, is one of the best precedents for the two-story type on the Island. Originally there was a gallery at the second floor level, as shown by the band, and the doorway giving out on this balcony has been replaced, patently, by a window. The entrance doorway has most interesting details, the door being made up of moulded battens, put in on the diagonal, like a barn door. Also, the cap and cornice merit attention, as do the shutters, which open only in the lower half, as the upper sash was fixed.

At Easthampton we have the Mulford House and the home of John Howard Payne, the author of "Home, Sweet Home." These houses, the Mulford and the Payne, built about 1660, are practically duplicates. They are shingled and

Detail of Doorway

HOUSE AT EAST MARION, LONG ISLAND

Detail of Porch

WEBB HOUSE, EAST MARION, LONG ISLAND

Detail of Doorway

HOUSE AT EAST MARION, LONG ISLAND

have low eaves and the cornices are plaster coves. The Payne House is excellently preserved and is a museum of interest. The interiors have panelings which must have been made by a ship's carpenter, so quaintly and delicately are they framed together.

The road from Greenport to Riverhead passes through the towns of Southold, New Suffolk, Cutchogue, Acquebogue and Laurel, all of which have numerous examples of delightful doorways.

Detail of Doorway

ANNA HALSEY HOUSE, WATERMILL, LONG ISLAND

At Southold, in addition, we find three examples of houses with dormers, a most unusual feature, for practically all the other houses on the eastern end of Long Island have unbroken roofs.

These little wood-built houses display a certain charm and picturesque quality that are not always found in Colonial work of greater pretension. Used as inspiration for modern work of modest character, they are of particular value in enabling the designer to make direct application of their scheme of composition without fear of losing that indefinable individuality which so frequently happens when the larger houses are reduced in scale.

THOMAS HALSEY HOUSE — c1800 — WATERMILL, LONG ISLAND

MACKAY HOUSE, SOUTHAMPTON, LONG ISLAND

OSBORNE (MOTT) HOUSE, BELLPORT, LONG ISLAND

WHITE HOUSE, NEAR WATERMILL, LONG ISLAND

WEBB HOUSE—c1790—EAST MARION, LONG ISLAND

Early Wood-Built Houses
of Central New York

Text by
Carl C. Tallman
Photographs by
The Author
Originally published in 1918 as White Pine Monograph
Volume IV, Number 5

Detail of Doorway
MILLER HOUSE, LUDLOWVILLE, NEW YORK

EARLY WOOD-BUILT HOUSES OF CENTRAL NEW YORK

IN the year 1828, prior to which time almost all of the post-Colonial buildings in central New York had been erected—for the Greek Revival had then begun to assert itself—a gentleman from Scotland, one James Stuart, accompanied by his wife, passed through this section upon the first leg of a three-years' tour covering most of the parts of the United States then inhabited.[1] To the author Mr. Stuart's narration of stage-coach episodes and his description of the villages of central New York seem to create an atmosphere of the early days which hardly could be equaled by a present day writer. Ninety years ago the villages must have presented a chaste and dignified appearance, unspoiled by motley groupings of almost all the known styles of architecture and "carpentecture" which in later years were planted heterogeneously amidst the unassuming post-Colonial structures. Probably the simple character of the villages was not greatly disturbed by the Classic Revival, which held sway until about 1845, although the de-

signers of that period aimed at more pretentious edifices. Their work, however, failed to possess that subtle charm which the earlier builders had managed to incorporate in their structures. It is not necessary to dwell at length upon the horrors that succeeded the decline of the Greek Revival and the lack of appreciation of the old work which became manifest when so-called modern improvements were introduced. Suffice it to say that from the author's observations the post-Colonial buildings of central New York have suffered more at the hands of "progress" than have those in any other section of the country.

Let us then go back to the early days, taking our seats upon the stage at Utica in company with our narrator:

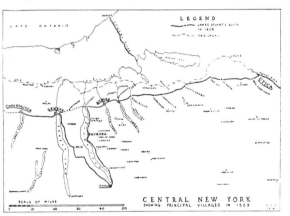

MAP OF CENTRAL NEW YORK
Showing James Stuart's Route

*From 30th of August to 1st of September, 1828.
From Utica to Auburn.*

"We found the stage partly filled before we prepared to take our seats,—half an hour before sunrise,—and did not reach Auburn[2] until nearly

---

[1] "Three Years in North America," by James Stuart. Published in Edinburg, 1833.

[2] The distance from Utica to Auburn is seventy-five miles.

sunset. The morning was very hot, but we had some welcome showers in the forenoon, after which the heat became much more tolerable, the road indifferent, and frequently not in the best line; but our charioteers drove pretty steadily at the rate of seven miles an hour. There were many wooden bridges over creeks—the name given to small rivers in this country—and

HOUSE AT VERNON CENTER, NEW YORK

the rapid driving of our cumbersome machine down the hills to those bridges was at first rather appalling; but the drivers got on so fearlessly, and at the same time seemed to have their horses so well in hand, that we very soon thought ourselves as safe as in an English stage coach. Our route led us through a good country, diversified with hill and dale, and considerable hollows— much excellent land, all cleared and settled within the last thirty or thirty-five years. We passed

many thriving villages,—towns we should call most of them: New Hartford, Manchester, Vernon, Oneida, Lenox, Chittenango, Manlius, Jamesville, Onondaga, Marcellus, and Skaneateles, adjoining a lake of the same name. The valley of Onondaga is exceedingly beautiful, and the town neat and clean looking, with a handsome opening and piece of fine sward in its center. We were in the neighborhood of two small settlements of Indians.[1] In one place, the children of the Indians followed the stage a long way to get a few cents from us. Everything has a thriving appearance in this district—crops good —and we have also today seen many patches of buckwheat. Farmhouses, generally with a portico, piazza, or balcony on one side, and a few locust trees or Lombardy poplars about the

[1] Onondaga Indian Reservation.

Photograph by Owen F. Scott

Rear Porch
HOUSE AT VERNON CENTER, NEW YORK

buildings, and in all cases large orchards at this season laden with fruit. Near the house, and sometimes in the orchards, is the burying-ground of the family, marked by the erection of a few gravestones.

"We breakfasted at Vernon, seventeen miles from Utica, this morning, and had even more than an abundant American breakfast set before us. Onondaga is the usual place for dining on

HOWARD SOULE HOUSE—1814—
SENNETT, CAYUGA COUNTY, NEW YORK

this journey; but a party of militia on duty there had, I presume, partaken of our dinner; for we were told that we must wait for some time. This we were unwilling to do; and, having got a lunch of cheese and bread, we delayed our chief meal until we reached the coffeehouse hotel at Auburn.

"Auburn itself is situated on the outlet of the Oswesco[1] Lake, conveniently for manufactures,

and is a thriving place, with a population of about 4000. It might have been the Auburn of Goldsmith, but for its numerous manufacturing establishments, and for its being the situation of one of the two great state prisons of the state of New York. There are printing offices, and various newspapers here, as at all the villages; one of the papers devoted entirely to religious discussion and intelligence.[2] There are several hotels; one of them, a splendid-looking house, contains about 200 beds.

"Nowhere in this country has there been a more complete change since the revolution, than in that part of it where we are now traveling, in point of general improvement of population, and the comforts of living and traveling."

Continuing with the diary:

---

[1] Owasco.

[2] Auburn Theological Seminary was founded in 1818.

HOUSE ON WEST SIDE OF SKANEATELES LAKE—1818—NEW YORK

HOUSE AT ELBRIDGE—1815—ONONDAGA COUNTY, NEW YORK

HOUSE, 544 SOUTH MAIN STREET, GENEVA, NEW YORK
Built by Dr. Mandeville, 1800–1818.

From 2nd September to 9th September.

"Soon after our visit to the Auburn prison,[1] we left the very comfortable family hotel at that village in the stage for Ithaca, at the head of the Cayuga Lake, in order to have a look at the village of Aurora, on the eastern side of the lake, and to see a little more of the lakes than we should if we had adhered to the direct western road, which passes the outlets or northern ends of those lakes. The lakes are parallel to each other, about thirty-three or thirty-five miles

houses, but a number of detached, clean-looking, and apparently comfortable small villas, enclosed in courts, or spots of garden ground ornamented with a few weeping willows or locust trees.

"We passed many good farms, some of them recently brought into cultivation, on which the usual processes of house-building, and enclosing by strong wooden rails, were in progress.

"Ithaca is a very flourishing village, the center of several great roads, with a population of between 3000 and 4000, and buildings in rapid progress.

MILLER HOUSE, LUDLOWVILLE, NEW YORK

long, and two miles broad; our route is by the eastern side of the Cayuga Lake to Ithaca, and thence by the western[2] side of Seneca Lake to Geneva on its northern extremity.

"We proceeded by the western road as far as the outlet from Cayuga Lake, where there is a wooden bridge remarkable for its length, above a mile, and thence by the east side of the lake to Aurora, which is charmingly situated on rising ground above the lake, and is considered an eligible place of residence, on account of the beauty of the surrounding scenery, and cheapness of the necessaries of life. The village does not consist of a connected street, or rows of

"We pursued our journey on the 5th towards Geneva. The only village we passed on our way to Geneva was Ovid, with its handsomely situated church, and fine piece of green turf between the church and hotel. The American villages are generally announced to you by the spires of their churches peeping through the trees.

"The situation of Geneva on a terrace above the lake is very delightful, as well as commanding, and the village, containing some good houses, and a population of 2000 or 3000, seems an agreeable place of residence, more cheerful looking, and the landscapes and views more pleasing, than any of our resting places since leaving the vale of the Mohawk.

"Early on the 7th September, we proceeded to Canandaigua, on the lake of the same name,

[1] Auburn prison built 1817.
[2] Mr. S. is in error here. A subsequent reference to the village of Ovid shows that the route was on the eastern side of Seneca Lake.

Detail of Side Elevation
PHELPS HOUSE—1813—NORTH MAIN STREET, CANANDAIGUA, NEW YORK

Front Elevation
GRANGER HOUSE — 1816 — NORTH MAIN STREET, CANANDAIGUA, NEW YORK

sixteen miles distant from Geneva, through a very fertile district; it is considered the most beautiful village in the state of New York; population about 3000. It rises gradually for above a mile from the lake, with an extensive opening for the public buildings in the center of the street. I am not sure, if I admire the situation more than that of Geneva, but the style of the houses is decidedly superior. There is more appearance of their having been designed and set down with taste than I have ever observed elsewhere. In short, advantage has been taken

ever. Second, where their charm has been appreciated—and consequently their original appearance preserved free from serious alterations—the early houses stand out as examples of domestic architecture worthy of becoming the source of inspiration for modern home-builders. Instances of such appreciation are to be seen in Canandaigua and Geneva perhaps to a greater extent than in other villages and cities, although here and there throughout the territory are to be found scattered examples which have been spared. No architect—in fact,

TWO HOUSES ON MILL STREET, ITHACA, NEW YORK

The one on the right was moved to its present location recently to clear original site for a business block.

of the ground, and of its relative situation with the lake, to place them on the fittest spots. They are generally separate and distinct dwelling-houses, their exterior painted perfectly white, and they recede from the street of the village, the sides of which are shaded with trees, enclosed in neatly laid out gardens. Some houses are large, and too good to be denominated villas."

Having caught a glimpse of the country and the principal villages as they appeared ninety years ago, let us rapidly retrace our journey in order to observe the present condition of the old houses. A careful survey today points out two facts very clearly. First, where roofs have been maintained reasonably weather-tight the old buildings invariably are found to be as sound as

no layman, if he possesses an interest in such matters, and it is evident on the whole that the layman's appreciation is continually increasing—should miss the opportunity of visiting Geneva and Canandaigua when he is in their vicinity. No guide is needed to point out the delightful old houses in these towns, but in the remainder of the territory the tourist must travel many miles always with his eyes wide open—for the interesting examples of early architecture are not always apparent to the casual observer. The interest of such a tour, however, is not confined to architecture, for the country in the vicinity of the Finger Lakes, with its combination of natural scenery and well-developed farms, is wonderfully beautiful.

THOMAS BEALS HOUSE—1815—NORTH MAIN STREET, CANANDAIGUA, NEW YORK

HOUSE ON SOUTH MAIN STREET, GENEVA, NEW YORK
Built in 1820 by Charles A. Williamson.

The oldest houses are to be found mostly on or near the original turnpike. Colonel Williamson (whose house at Geneva is illustrated herein) is authority for the following in reference to the road from Utica, via Cayuga ferry and Canandaigua, to the Genesee River at Avon: "This line of road having been established by law, not less than fifty families settled upon it in the space of four months after it was opened." Though the road was probably laid out in 1794, it seems not to have been constructed for some time, for in June, 1797, Col. Williamson represents the road from Fort Schuyler to the Genesee as little better than an Indian trail. It was,

main road east and west follows the old turnpike the greater part of the distance, but from Chittenango to Auburn the present state road lies to the north of the old route, passing through Syracuse, which in the days before the Erie Canal was but a small hamlet reached by a spur of the old road from Onondaga. Upon the completion of the Erie Canal in 1825, villages naturally sprang up along its banks. The early architectural development in these villages, however, lacked the charm of the earlier work along the turnpike.

The author will not attempt a classification, or division into periods, of the many variations

DR. CARR-HAYES HOUSE — 1826 — GIBSON STREET, CANANDAIGUA, NEW YORK

however, so far improved subsequently, that on the 30th day of September, 1799, a stage started from Utica and arrived at Genesee in the afternoon of the third day, and from that period it is believed that a regular stage has passed between these two places. In the year 1800, a law was enacted by the legislature of the state for making this road a turnpike. The work of construction was commenced without delay, and completed in a short time.

The work illustrated herein has been selected mainly from that part of the country which lies near the old turnpike, following Mr. Stuart's deviation around Cayuga Lake. Today the

of style which are to be found in this territory. As a result of the diversified origin of the early settlers, one sees evidences that the early builders were inspired by Colonial buildings in various older settlements nearer tidewater, from New England to Maryland and Virginia. While buildings of frame construction predominate, many old stone and brick structures, with white pine trim, are to be found.

The author hopes that the few examples herein illustrated will help to bring about a closer study of the early buildings of central New York, so that their story may be added to the records of Colonial and post-Colonial research.

BALDWIN HOUSE—1838—SOUTH STREET, AUBURN, NEW YORK

BOODY HOUSE—1835—ROSE HILL ON SENECA LAKE, OPPOSITE GENEVA, NEW YORK

Detail of Doorway
HOUSE AT VERNON, NEW YORK

The Greek Revival in Owego

Text by
Alexander B. Trowbridge
Photographs by
Kenneth Clark
Originally published in 1921 as White Pine Monograph
Volume VII, Number 3

VESPER CLIFF (JOHNSON-PLATT HOUSE) — 1830 — OWEGO, NEW YORK

THE GREEK REVIVAL IN OWEGO AND NEARBY NEW YORK TOWNS

YOU may think it strange that one should hesitate to write for so excellent a publication as *The White Pine Series*, but possibly you have not fully taken in the title of this chapter. I was asked to write about some old houses in Owego and nearby towns in the southern part of central New York, and, frankly and architecturally speaking, I had never heard of them. To be sure, I knew there were some old residences in Owego, built in 1830 or 1840, but, in common with most of my professional colleagues, I had never given them more than a passing glance. We architects as a class are peculiar in that once we make up our minds that a certain style or period is discredited by the profession, we "praise it with faint damns," if we speak of it at all. It may be that we are snobs, professionally, in not taking up with the Greek Revival, for example, and trying to evolve from it a style or a treatment which, when purged of the faults which are so evident, might result in an attractive residence architecture.

The editor was clever in sending as his emissary a young lady whose family for generations had lived in Owego and who knew so much about these old houses that she made me feel that I ought to write about them for my own good. And so here I am driving away at an article, surrounded by notes culled from a ponderous volume on the history of Tioga County, and by numerous photographs of the early architecture of that section of New York State.

What a wonderful place is the big library! When an employee is engaged to give out books it must be that a clause is inserted in the agreement stipulating "courtesy is the essence of this contract." As I handed in my application slip for a history of Tioga County, my thoughts naturally turned to the earlier, more inviting periods of American architecture, when men were courtly and dressed the part. Their homes harmonized with their costumes. The architecture and the accompanying furnishings seem at this distance to have been perfectly in keeping with the social life of the time. There was a dignity, a repose befitting the life of a country gentleman, which is expressed in those old homes of New England and Virginia. At any rate, as I was on my quest and was surrounded by thousands of cubic feet of condensed wisdom, I had forgotten for the moment my former reluctance to write this chapter and was on my toes with expectancy. Well—what did I find? Instead of the powdered wigs, the satin breeches, the big silver-buckled shoes, and "Zounds, Gadzooks," and all that sort of thing, I found—I might have known it if I had thought at all—the frock coat donned for daguerreotypes, the heavy boots of native cobbling, and, most disconcerting of all, whiskers which the Goldberg type of humorist likes to draw. Here was a nice situation. Can any one write upon an architecture connected with so unlovely a period? Think how different it would be to descant upon the good old days when precious china graced the tea ceremonies, and lovely hand-wrought silver was no curiosity but held its dignified place in hundreds of charming homes. In those days they had perfectly trained servants who could mix as well as serve. Think what we have come to when we have difficulty in getting any kind of servants and are not any longer permitted to mix! And they had their graceful and courtly minuet with its quaint music, which also seemed to fit perfectly the china, the furniture, the wall papers, etc. Is it absurd to assert that all these elements combined to create a naïve charm which is, after all, the essence of American Colonial? In the big book on Tioga County there were no references to things graceful or courtly. It was a farming country, the kind which furnishes the backbone of America. And when Abraham Lincoln called for volunteers to defend the Union, Tioga County was one of those communities which came to the scratch. But farming and patriotism — even when they are of the highest order — do not necessarily produce good architecture, and the houses of 1830 or 1840 reflected, as architecture always does, the degree of development of the people of that place and period.

That portion of New York which we are to discuss was, in the beginning, the habitat of the Iroquois tribes, the Oneidas, Mohawks, Cayugas, Senecas, Onondagas, etc. Tioga, the county in which the town of Owego sleeps, was given an Indian name meaning "at the forks," and was pronounced Te-yo-ge-ga by the Mohawks. Simplified spelling — which many suppose is a modern science — came to the rescue in those early days, the latter part of the eighteenth century, and Ti-o-ga it has been ever since. If something like simplified spelling could be introduced into architectural design, how much better our modern buildings would be! At any rate, in 1785, when Thomas Jefferson in Virginia was experimenting with snake-like brick fences and was making a national reputation as an authority on classic architecture, the only habitation on the site of the present town of Owego was a log cabin built and occupied by Amos Draper. Now, if I may be pardoned for reviving a painful subject, a distillery was erected in Tioga County in 1800, though it was not until forty-four years later that the first

Detail of Doorway
HOLLENBECK HOUSE, FRONT STREET
OWEGO, NEW YORK

temperance organization of that section came into existence. The history states that six hard drinkers became conscience-smitten and formed this society to protect the good name of the community. One authority declares they feared all the liquor would be consumed unless someone took steps to reduce the consumption of the public and private stock, and that this temperance society was the logical expression of this fear. These theories do not appeal to me, for I am convinced that the introduction of Greek ornament in the houses built about this time was the true cause of the temperance movement. If you study the embellishment on the Hollenbeck House on Front Street in Owego, you will see what I mean. The story goes that those same hard drinkers were returning one clear moonlight night from the "Lodge," and as they passed the Hollenbeck House they saw certain queer shapes frisking on the roof just above the eaves. Each one of the six was greatly startled but did not dare speak of the matter to any of the others. The next day they were all much relieved to note that what had frightened them so thoroughly was only a touch of the Greek Revival. The experience sobered them and the temperance society followed. The two porches to the right and left of the portico were added later, and, while history says nothing about them, it is very clear that they were derived from the teepee or wigwam style of architecture, doubtless as a compliment to the original owners of the land.

Why the citizens of this section of our country chose pseudo-Greek architecture translated rather unintelligently into wood is a secret that disappeared with the whiskers. It is clear, however, that the finest homes of that period indicated the approval of the Greek Revival by the best families.

Why does the average educated architect dismiss the Greek Revival with a shrug? Is it not because he notes that the translation from the stone architecture of classic days to a white pine treatment was merely badly done? Porticoes and pediments were given the scale of stone architecture, and the instinctive feeling for good wooden scale seemingly did not exist. There is no reason why Greek mouldings and Greek ornament should not be charmingly used today in wood architecture if the same respect for materials is shown which controlled the builders of good Colonial houses. In Colonial work we are perfectly aware of the classic origin, but we are not conscious of imitation. The charm of that style lies in the naïve

examine these photographs, therefore, to see whether really useful ideas cannot be gleaned from them.

The Hollenbeck House would be greatly improved by removing entirely the meaningless ornament nailed to the roof as a kind of snow guard. An architect who was studying design in Paris about twenty years ago was heard to remark, "I believe we should decorate where there's something doing"—a slangy way of expressing a great truth. Surely the snow guard referred to does not illustrate this principle. The

HOLLENBECK HOUSE, FRONT STREET, OWEGO, NEW YORK

adaptation of a masonry architecture.

Lest this chapter should take on the appearance of a little slam, let me state that I have no desire to be unkind to my subject. When, however, one sees a clumsy attempt to execute in painted wood the proportions and the details of the lovely creations of the Periclean age, one cannot resist the impulse to poke fun at it. But is it not possible that, following the lead of the Colonial architects, we might be able to evolve delightful wooden houses by a use of Greek mouldings and Greek ornament controlled by an intelligent respect for our material? Let us

two wigwam porches also could be removed, greatly to the enhancement of the ensemble. A careful study of the portico cornice discloses a group of clumsy mouldings. The use of the Greek ornament in a form suggesting a low pediment is not bad per se, but it appears beaten down and looks as though a restudy in its relation to the portico entablature would greatly improve its ornamental value, particularly if the entire entablature were reduced in both width and height. The architrave appears not to stand over the outer line of the column at the upper diameter, but projects beyond, Greek fashion,

MACKAY HOUSE, WILLSEYVILLE, NEW YORK

thereby producing a heaviness which is not pleasing. Here is where strict subservience to Greek methods was unwise and the Roman custom would have been preferable.

The Mackay House in Willseyville is a very good example of the Greek Revival at its best, *i.e.*, there are evidences of book knowledge of Greek proportions and Greek mouldings, but the scale is so heavy as to interfere with the home-like, domestic character which a residence should possess. Who wants to live in a Greek temple, anyway? There are no interior photographs to accompany these views, but one can picture the haircloth sofas, the braided hair ornaments, the wax flowers in glass cases, the front parlor used only for funerals and weddings, the heavy walnut furniture, and the kerosene lamps everywhere! I see the frock coat, the alfalfa whiskers, the Irish upper lip, and the stern insistence upon selected reading and no music on Sundays. This has nothing particularly to do with the merits and defects of these houses, except that the austerity of the architecture is without doubt a reflection of the stiffness of the social life. Very likely the original owners of these formal and rather stately residences followed classical studies at Harvard or Yale or Union or Middlebury, and Greek architecture may have been the natural form of expression which followed those classical studies.

Suppose, now, we could redesign this house, without altering its plan. Would we not remove the immense entablatures on the wings, give a lighter touch to the main entablature of the portico, lighten somewhat the columns, refine the composition and the mouldings at the main entrance, and in every way give to the house a wood scale? As the design now stands, it could be done in stone without these changes, and while a stone treatment would not result in a residential flavor, it would at least produce a more consistent architecture.

Vesper Cliff in Owego is saved by the splendid trees which shut out portions of the house and throw shadows of lovely pattern upon those portions which are exposed to view. It seems hypercritical to find fault with a picture which has so much in it that is beautiful. But we must keep in mind that this is a residence, while it exhibits the solidity and the scale of a court house. The photograph discloses a custom which also appears in the Daniels House in Owego and in the Mill Street house in Ithaca, which the writer does not recall having seen in modern work, but which gives a certain charm in surprise, *i.e.,* the smooth surfaced wall behind the veranda columns, which contrasts in an interesting way with the clapboard treatment on the end. This is reversed in the Daniels House, where the smooth surface is on the end. In the Ithaca

DANIELS HOUSE, MAIN STREET,
OWEGO, NEW YORK

house a combination of the two is shown. Is there not in this little suggestion much that is fruitful? Is not the central motive of the Ithaca house greatly benefited by the framing which it receives from the horizontal lines of the clapboards on each side? In Vesper Cliff the writer prefers the shadows on the smooth wall to those which fall on the siding. They seem to present a decoration more happily than they do on the end where the leafy shadows are rudely cut by the horizontal lines of the clapboarding.

The Daniels House looks like something which

HOUSE AT 106 WATER STREET, ITHACA, NEW YORK

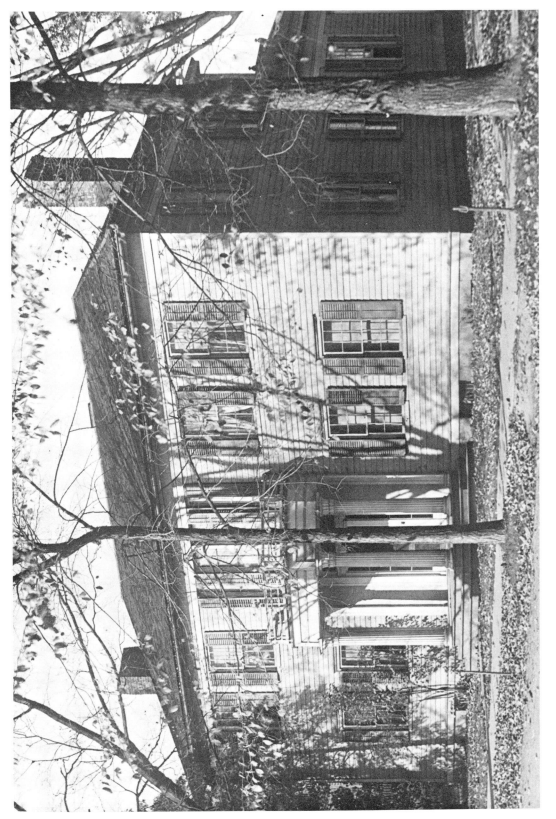

DOWNS HOUSE, FRONT STREET, OWEGO, NEW YORK

started out to be dressed in the costume of the Greek Revival, but weakened at the last moment and fell back upon pseudo-Colonial details. It would take a seer to trace the origin of the detail of the main pilasters. Perhaps the inspiration came from mantelpieces, for there are many which show this Egyptian-like group of stems. Has any one in modern times tried this detail on large pilasters filling the entire panel instead of merely the middle third? It might

Nichols, Tioga County, and in the country between Owego and Nichols, are curious and rather interesting examples of the influence of both Dutch and Colonial work. The elliptical arches are probably inspired from Dutch brick buildings built near Syracuse. The cornice and pediment in the Nichols House are near Colonial. The window trim in the latter house shows true Colonial origin though it has the scale of a bedroom mantelpiece. The rosettes at the necks

HOUSE ON ROAD BETWEEN OWEGO AND NICHOLS, NEW YORK

be made an effective substitute for the classic flutings which are the resort of the unimaginative. The modillions are obviously too short to give the appearance of doing effectively the work entrusted to them. The rake mouldings of the pediment do not return on the side of the building and their place is taken by a metal gutter. It is, of course, possible that the original gutter was of wood and that the continued concentration of moisture rotted the gutter while other sections of the cornice remained intact.

The next two houses, built in the town of

of the pilasters have a true Colonial flavor. The purist deplores the arch turned in wood, but there can be no real objection to a treatment of the kind shown when the thickness of the arch is obviously too thin for anything except wood. It might have been better if the space between the top of the arch and the bed moulding of the cornice had been a little greater in each of these houses, merely to satisfy the eye. The house at Nichols was built by settlers who emigrated from New England. This accounts for the excellence of the detail, which, while not

HOUSE AT NICHOLS, NEW YORK

up to the grade of the best Colonial work, is much better than the average in Tioga County. The house between Owego and Nichols, while less good in its mouldings and smaller details, contains architectural workmanship superior to that of the Nichols House. Note the wider space between the two middle pilasters and compare it with the even spacing in the Nichols House. Note also the skillful way in which the corner is handled (see detail photograph on page 95),

House, increased a little, in scale. How would it do to try the smooth wall surface on the main front, particularly as a field or background to these rather delicate window trims? One more thing—in any treatment in which elliptical arches are to take the place, on the front, of what otherwise would be a nearly completed entablature, would it not look much better not to have this horizontal fascia with bed moulding carry clear across the building at its maximum

Detail

HOUSE AT NICHOLS, NEW YORK

where surfaces are placed to receive returning mouldings and clapboards, and things look thought out. Now why not venture a modern house on the following lines: A principal motive composed somewhat like the house last referred to. The general conception of the detailing would follow the detail photograph, but the mouldings of pilaster cap, of cornice, and of pediment would be studied from good Colonial sources. The space over the arches might be increased and the trim around the windows might follow the type shown in the Nichols

projection? I would much prefer to reduce this cornice member to the point where it would merely act as a cap moulding to the surface which is arched. This can be accomplished by returning this cornice member to the wall shortly after it turns the corner.

The Ithaca house has a charm all its own, but it lacks a setting. It needs trees and leafy shadows. The wood scale is delightfully felt and the contrast between the clapboards and the matched siding gives a happy effect. The window trim is nothing but a plain board which, when

Detail of Pilaster and Pediment
HOUSE ON ROAD BETWEEN OWEGO AND
NICHOLS, NEW YORK

Detail of Pilaster and Pediment
DANIELS HOUSE, OWEGO, NEW YORK

Detail of Doorway

DOWNS HOUSE, OWEGO, NEW YORK

Detail of Doorway

MACKAY HOUSE, WILLSEYVILLE, NEW YORK

the blinds are open, is mainly covered up. This plain trim is entirely effective, for the proportions of the windows are good and a more elaborate trim is not required. An examination of the detail photograph on page 98 of the entrance discloses a quaint scheme of carrying the flutes of the pilasters into the archivolt. The recessed door gives a sense of solidity to the construction, which almost looks like a trick to imitate stonework. It was undoubtedly derived from stone or brick architecture and is saved by the way the wood is treated on the face and in the jambs.

The Downs House in Owego is the last one to be mentioned, perhaps from an instinctive habit of reserving the best for the last. Here is a house which contains that subtle charm arising from good proportion which is a thing not to be defined or formulated. When it is done we pick out the things which explain the happy result—such as an entablature which is just right for wood architecture. The windows are grouped so as to give good sturdy corner wall spaces. The window trim is ornamented only at the top—where the trim shows. The roof is unspoiled by dormer windows and therefore helps to accentuate the simplicity of the whole. I would add that the portico is not worthy of imitation. The capitals suggest the Greek Revival, as if the house is, in the main, much older

than the porch. The entablature and railing of the portico are crude, and the two outer columns do not seem properly related to the corners of the half octagon which they support. The portico entablature suggests, however, the very great relief to be found in devising this element of the building without resort to the cut-and-dried architrave frieze and cornice. A simple architrave for structural appearance, a modified frieze, and a very much modified cornice consisting of bed mould and a projecting drip moulding, are all that the portico needs, to give it its proper relative importance. As it now stands, the portico is a bit out of scale with the rest of the house, and not as well worked out.

We may assume that those houses having entrances at one side have stairs also at the side and a hall bedroom over the entrance hall. Those like the Downs House very probably have the hall running through the house with a door on the rear end opening into a garden. This type of plan was commonly used at the beginning of the nineteenth century, and is most livable and homelike if appropriately furnished. It is doubtful if we could learn much even if we had plans drawn to scale, for the plan arrangements would in no sense be different from hundreds of other houses of the period, and not as good as the Colonial places evolved a half-century earlier.

VESPER CLIFF, OWEGO, NEW YORK

Detail of Doorway
HOUSE AT 106 WATER STREET, ITHACA, NEW YORK

Old Chatham, New York

Text by
Alwyn T. Covell
Photographs by
Kenneth Clark
Originally published in 1919 as White Pine Monograph
Volume V, Number 5

Detail of Entrance and Front Façade
HOUSE AT CHATHAM CENTER, NEW YORK

OLD CHATHAM AND
NEIGHBORING DWELLINGS
SOUTH OF THE BERKSHIRES

ONE of the most interesting peculiarities of early American domestic architecture is its "localism," its adherence to type within the confines, often, of a very restricted locality.

There are, of course, the broad, general divisions of types, or styles, with which we are generally familiar—the domestic architecture of the New England states, of the Middle Atlantic states, and of the South.

These broad divisions, however, would by no means serve to identify all early American dwellings, because there were substyles, and distinctly local styles, many of which were radically at variance with the "typical example."

In the South, for instance, all the great houses did not have classic colonnaded porticoes. Besides the Creole type of the far South (a type absolutely peculiar to the locality), there were a great many differing varieties of the style of the Classic Revival, and there were also the detached houses found in Richmond, Charleston, Norfolk, Annapolis, Alexandria, Baltimore and elsewhere in Delaware, Maryland, Virginia and the Carolinas. All could be classed as "Southern," but there are wide differences in their characteristics.

In the Middle Atlantic states there are the varieties developed by the early pioneer settlers of Pennsylvania as well as by its later more prosperous families. Different, again, is the farmhouse of the Dutch colonists, who built in the northern part of New Jersey, on Staten Island and Long Island, through New York State well up into the Mohawk Valley, and, on the west bank of the Hudson, throughout the Ramapo Hills and the Catskills.

In New England is found further variety, with widely different types, seen in isolated farmhouses and in the substantial homes of the merchants and ship-owners of Salem, Newport and New Bedford.

It is the purpose of this chapter, however, to show how a particular type of house, its identity traceable through detail, appears scattered in an irregular line southward from the Berkshires to the vicinity of Danbury, in Connecticut. And a remarkable proof of the close localism of early American types of domestic architecture is seen in the fact that the examples illustrated, although found but a few miles from Litchfield, possess characteristics pronouncedly different.

A departure of a few miles from Connecticut is made in the inclusion of the unusually interesting houses in and near Old Chatham, which is over the New York state line due west from Pittsfield and Lenox, and due northwest from Stockbridge and Great Barrington, Massachusetts.

It is permissible, however, to include these Old Chatham houses with the Connecticut examples found at Sharon, Kent, Danbury and adjacent townships, because their architectural affinity is at once apparent.

The houses show far more imagination and sophistication in matters of detail than those of Litchfield, the use of Palladian windows being the most conspicuous common feature. Nothing in Litchfield, however, resembles the fine old house at Chatham Center shown in the illustrations on pages 100, 102, 103, and 106.

This house and others included in this chapter show a marked tendency to develop the design of the entrance by the elaboration of the porch. Fanlights and sidelights were frequently used, and the Palladian window above the entrance appears to have been the *sine qua non* of the really pretentious house of this type.

It was also a favorite device to plaster the under side of the hood in the forms of cylindrical or elliptical barrel vaults, instead of the plastered quarter-spherical treatment of typical Pennsylvania origin, the Germantown hood. It would seem, further, that it was the fashion to paint the plaster in these early Connecticut porch-vaults (including the Chatham, New York, examples) a rich shade of blue.

strict classicism, as is apparent not only in the carefree disregard of the traditional relationship of the members of a classic entablature, but in such quaint vagaries as the continuous fringe of reguli, alternating long and short, with no attempt at triglyphs to relate them to the guttae of the projection immediately above.

With a thorough knowledge of classic precedents and proportions, it would probably be quite impossible to make the naïve departures from rule which, in the case of these early master-carpenters, were crowned and peculiar success.

For the preservation of these delightful evi-

Detail of Entablature and Window Head
HOUSE AT CHATHAM CENTER, NEW YORK

Most interesting of all, however, is a study of the detail of these houses—detail of which the precedent is lost in obscurity. Certainly some echo of Georgian feeling reached these builders, yet their execution and their departures from academic forms suggest that the Georgian influence was not had at first hand. The bas-relief urns and sunbursts in the frieze of the house at Chatham Center certainly recall the style of the brothers Adam, as does also the strong leaning toward elliptical forms, but the manner in which these are carried out is one of extreme architectural naïveté.

The cornices are distinctly classic in general character, but again depart vigorously from any

dences of architectural ingenuousness, it is fortunate that the builders of our early days carried out virtually all their work in white pine, which has held its form without disintegration for the successive decades in which no protective coats of paint have rejuvenated the gray and weather-beaten exteriors.

It is probable, however, the builders of these old houses, especially of those which display a profusion of detail, favored white pine because of the ease with which clear mouldings could be run from it, and because of its receptiveness to the carver's tool.

In the gable end of one of the wings of the Chatham Center house are seen planks of ex-

traordinary width. In many respects this old house affords rich material for study. The treatment of the windows and of the corner pilasters shows a high degree of architectural instinct, when we realize, in the whole house, ample evidence of a lack of academic architectural knowledge. The presence of strong architectural instinct is felt, also, in the whole mass of the house, for no architect of today would hesitate to admit that the management of gabled wings, flush with the main façade, is a difficult problem. Few, indeed, would attempt to under-

the manner of dentils, as a purely decorative treatment of the window heads. The square-headed Palladian window over the porch is excellent in proportion, and well in character with the breadth and amplitude apparent in the whole design.

Traveling southward from Chatham, and back over the state line into Connecticut, but a few miles from Litchfield, Sharon is found to possess a number of very interesting houses. These, for the most part, are more developed in detail than the Litchfield houses, the scale of the

Cornice Detail
HOUSE AT CHATHAM CENTER, NEW YORK

take such a problem, and fewer still would achieve so successful a result.

The Harper House, at Old Chatham, presents a distinctly graceful porch, and another instance of bas-relief sunbursts in the frieze, strangely unrelated to the windows immediately below, but highly interesting in itself.

The third house, found near Old Chatham, is an unusually interesting one, conspicuous, as a "four-square" mass, for its admirably dignified and static proportions. Its siding boards are not lapped, but flush (an unusual detail for this locality), but its detail is closely in character with other houses in the vicinity. The entablature follows a more nearly classic formula, with its frieze detailed in a way to suggest triglyphs and metopes, though reguli are used, almost in

dentils and mouldings of the house illustrated on page 105 being unusually fine.

The embellishment of the frieze, seen in the old house at Chatham, is also apparent in Sharon, the detail of the house on page III being most effective.

Another interesting frieze treatment is seen in the Bacon House, at Kent, Connecticut — a house also possessing a number of other features. Especially interesting is the little rear porch, with tapered square posts, and the elaborate treatment of all the window heads. In the frieze, which is carried not only across the gable ends, but up into the peaks as well, there has been an evident intention of following classic precedent in the suggestion of triglyphs, though the alternate spaces are too narrow for metopes.

Detail of Entrance Porch and Front Façade
HARPER HOUSE, OLD CHATHAM, NEW YORK

Detail of Entrance
HOUSE AT SHARON, CONNECTICUT

HOUSE NEAR OLD CHATHAM, NEW YORK

BACON HOUSE, KENT, CONNECTICUT

The curious half-circles in the upper part of these spaces must have been meant to create, by their shadows, the effect of festoons.

At Danbury are found several houses of similar type—especially similar in the general design and detail of the porches. At Sandy Hook, in Connecticut, however, the resemblance swings far more closely toward the kind of house characteristic of Litchfield—plain, clapboarded, sitting close to the grade, and with entrance doors approached only by a broad stone step, and no porch.

Much of the interesting quality of Colonial

tectural genius. Many were downright stupid, but most of them, if we are to judge from their works, were strangely endowed with an inherent sense of architectural fitness.

Not all their detail was developed from books, though such famous works as *The Country Builder's Assistant* had wide popularity. Such forms, however, as may have been found in the *Assistant*, and other similar works, are often seen to have been only the basis upon which the more imaginative country builder developed a remarkable variety of individual interpretations.

If these American builders had known more

BACON HOUSE, KENT, CONNECTICUT

and early American domestic architecture, especially in localities remote from the more sophisticated and resourceful cities, came from the fact that nearly all the carpenters and builders in those days were their own architects as well.

There were but few men professionally practicing architecture apart from the actual building of the houses they were designing, and this made possible much of the peculiar kind of individuality characterizing our early domestic architecture.

Perhaps we instinctively admire the successes and ignore the failures of these early builders, which is both a natural and a generous thing to do. Certainly every country builder was by no means gifted with even a faint spark of archi-

about architectural precedent, or had known less than they did, their works would have been of a nature considerably different from the examples which survive.

But we cannot very well reckon their work in terms of architectural *knowledge*; these early builders had a thing which is, perhaps, rarer today—a keen and vigorous architectural *instinct*.

It was this that saved much of their work from being either grotesque or stupid, and which gave it many qualities which could never have been attained through mere architectural knowledge—qualities which afford a wealth and variety of inspiration to those architects of today who turn to early American types for the rendering of the modern American home.

Detail of Side Doorway
BACON HOUSE, KENT, CONNECTICUT

HOUSE AT SANDY HOOK, CONNECTICUT

ANOTHER HOUSE AT SANDY HOOK, CONNECTICUT

HOUSE AT SHARON, CONNECTICUT

JACKSON FARM, NEAR SHARON, CONNECTICUT

Entrance Detail
HOUSE IN WEST STREET, DANBURY, CONNECTICUT

Suffield, Connecticut

Text by
David E. Tarn
Photographs by
Kenneth Clark
Originally published in 1921 as White Pine Monograph
Volume VII, Number 6

Detail of Doorway
HOUSE AT SUFFIELD, CONNECTICUT

THE TOWN OF SUFFIELD, CONNECTICUT

THE villages and towns of New England, elm-shaded, with glimpses of white houses through the green, seem always to have deep roots in our national traditions and consciousness. And New England, too, has associations even more intimate in the minds of most of us, for there are few American families who cannot trace an ancestor who came from a village or town of New England. There is a spirit, certainly, of these early settlers which has widely affected our whole national temperament; New England is our point of departure, no matter how far from its elmshaded streets many ambitious pioneers have moved and settled.

And it is New England that gives us, as the symbol and type of the American home, the old, familiar "white house with the green blinds." Regardless of the many and varied kinds of houses we build, to satisfy architectural whims, that early tradition of the "white house with the green blinds" is never entirely absent from our thoughts or from our instinctive desires.

New England possesses, in a subtle but compelling way, a complete difference from any other part of the country. Although its spirit is manifest in our national temperament, and in much of our national instinct, New England lies very definitely on the Connecticut side of a state line and New York on the other. The demarcation is almost as distinct as the difference in color on the map.

In Connecticut there are many quiet inland villages and towns which easily escape discovery by the architectural explorer. They are off the beaten track, and have none of the wide familiarity of the well known seaport towns and much visited inland places of Massachusetts and Rhode Island.

Driving from Hartford to Springfield, follow-ing the Connecticut River northward, and north from Windsor Locks, the road will run through the old town of Suffield, which was founded in 1670. Proud of its Pilgrim pedigree, the people of Suffield produced an elaborate historical pageant in October, 1920, in commemoration of the settlement, and recalled the dauntless band of Pilgrims who came from Leyden in Holland, whither they had fled to escape persecution in England. Their leader, Major Pynchon, bought the land for the settlement for thirty pounds from the local Indian chieftain. Pampunkshat, and the first Suffield Town meeting was held in 1682.

A typical bit of New England history, this brief chronicle of the achievement of a group of determined colonists, who turned a wilderness into a town in less than twelve years. They wrought industriously and untiringly with their hands, and must have possessed a will to survive and to progress almost unbelievable in our present era of easy methods and ready-made necessities.

And what, besides their share of colonizing New England and their share in the immortal spirit of New England, did they leave for us to look upon today?

The first houses, of course, have disappeared, replaced by their builders and their children as prosperity increased and the struggle for mere existence became less engrossing. One of the oldest houses in Suffield is the Gay Manse, which bears the date 1742, a sturdy, gambrel-roofed house of the old New England type that followed those earliest ones, in which sharply pointed roof and overhanging second story were features brought directly over from Elizabethan England. Few of that earliest type remain, and relatively few of the first gambrel-roofed New

England houses such as this relic of old Suffield.

The Gay Manse is an unusually good example of its type, in proportion, in the contour of its roof, and in the spirit of its detail. The doorway, surmounted by a broken cyma pediment, is in admirable scale with the entire building, and, as a study by itself, reveals no less nicety of scale in its mouldings and parts. The incised "stone joints" of the jambs and lintels suggest the manner of the old State House in Newport, Rhode Island, as well as the graceful pediment, and it is by no means improbable that Newport may have been the source of inspiration. It is even possible that the pilasters, pediments, and mouldings may have been made in Newport, for there were many skilled woodworkers there whose doorways and mantels are found throughout Rhode Island. Be its origin what it may, it is a fine doorway, perhaps the most perfect, architecturally, in all Suffield.

Along the shaded main street there stands another gambrel-roofed house, known to have been built about 1736 by Captain Abraham Burbank. It is a little more pretentious than the old Gay Manse, more elaborate in its detail. It has wooden quoins after the manner of many of the finer houses of Salem and Newport. The main cornice is elaborated with block modillions and the first-story window heads are elaborated with a moulded entablature, with dentils, and a convex frieze. Two entrances afford further opportunity for studying detail. The first is a plain pediment porch, on Tuscan columns, with a triglyph frieze, apparently older than the entrance in the wing, which has a pediment over

Detail of Doorway
GAY MANSE, SUFFIELD, CONNECTICUT

a fanlight, on Composite columns and sidelights. The treatment of the entablature of this second door, however, is identical with that of the windows, which contradicts to some extent the theory of its later date. The entablature, of course, could have been copied, or, if both doors actually were built at the same time, there is nothing in precedent to say that it would have been impossible for one to have been designed with Tuscan and the other with Composite columns.

The wing to the left is apparently a later addition, but even the Dutch Colonial appearance of its roof does not detract from the essentially New England look of the Burbank House. It is a typical example of its style, conservative, dignified, and very expressive of simple domesticity.

The third gambrel-roofed house illustrated is the Thomas Archer Place, built about 1795. It is a far more modest affair than the Burbank House, but offers a considerable architectural enigma. The location of the two doors by no means suggests a rational plan within, and the doors themselves seem to be a part of some much more pretentious house. The door on the end with no steps or approach, or any other apparent reason for being so strangely placed, is in itself a distinguished piece of design, beautiful in detail and exceptionally fine in proportion. The entablature of this doorway, as well as that of the windows, is very similar to the window entablature of the Burbank House, and its date of building must fall nearly in the same year.

Another half-century saw marked differences in the Suffield citizens' idea of a suitable house. Again the name of "Gay," this time in the local

GAY MANSE—1742—SUFFIELD, CONNECTICUT

Detail of Window
GAY MANSE, SUFFIELD, CONNECTICUT

designation of Gay Mansion, built by Ebenezer King in 1795. Much more sophistication is
evident: the builder was by no means unfamiliar
with the "grand houses" of Salem and New-
buryport.

An architrave and frieze make, with the cornice, a complete entablature, which carries
around the building, and tall paneled pilasters,
two stories high, support it. The main evidence
of a greater sophistication is seen in the Palladian window, which was evidently so highly
regarded by the builder that he was inspired
to somewhat destroy its scale and importance
as a feature by making a very much smaller
one in the pediment, where there was only room
for a fanlight. Both entrances are very like
the second doorway of the Burbank House, and
there is also practically an identity in the archi-
traves of the windows on the first floor. This
whole house, substantially four-square and dignified, is "New England" architecturally per-
sonified.

A third type of roof is seen in the Captain
Phelps House, also built in 1795. It is the
plain "barn roof," the characteristic Connec-
ticut roof, of which so many are to be seen in
Litchfield and elsewhere throughout the state.
The Phelps House acquires dignity by means of

the tall corner pilasters, and centers its architectural interest mainly in its porch and Palladian window. The porch is a simple Ionic one,
with interesting mouldings in its entablature
and pediment. The Burbank House would seem
to have set a style in window heads, for here,
again, are the same convex frieze and the same
mouldings.

The Charles Shepard House is distinguished by
its very graceful porch, of which the balustrade,
however, would appear to be a later addition.
The general proportions of this house, and especially the pitch of the roof, are distinctly of
Connecticut.

Another interesting house (again with the
Burbank House window heads) shows a quaint
delusion on the part of its builder, who evidently believed that if one porch is desirable,
two would be doubly so, which led him to pile
one on top of the other. The effect is not a
happy one, and destroys the unity which the
street front would have if the builder had not
been so mistakenly profuse. This house, built
by Harvey Bissell in 1815, eighty years after
the Burbank House, also has rusticated wooden
quoins, and, as above mentioned, the same win-

Detail of Window
HARVEY BISSELL HOUSE,
SUFFIELD, CONNECTICUT

THOMAS ARCHER PLACE, SUFFIELD, CONNECTICUT
Known to have been lived in by Thomas Archer in 1795.

CAPTAIN ABRAHAM BURBANK HOUSE—1736—SUFFIELD, CONNECTICUT

GAY MANSION, SUFFIELD, CONNECTICUT
Built by Ebenezer King in 1795.

dow heads. The porte-cochère at the left is very evidently an addition of the "Chamfered Corner" period of the 1880's. In 1812 gambrel roofs had given place to the plain barn roof, but the device of carrying the clapboard side walls down to the grade with no foundation exposed is a much earlier and very characteristic New England custom.

There is an interesting quality in nearly all the early houses of Connecticut which differentiates them from those of other parts of New England, especially from the Massachusetts houses near Boston and the Rhode Island houses near Newport and Providence. The early Connecticut builders were very unsophisticated, and worked with far less actual knowledge of architectural detail than many of their contemporaries elsewhere. It is easy, for this reason, to find many mistakes and solecisms, but these seem more often to add interest to than to detract from their work.

Architecture in the United States enjoyed, in its early days, certain advantages which do not exist today. Natural limitations of stylistic influence existed, and while many may think of Colonial and early American builders as de-

Palladian Window

GAY MANSION, SUFFIELD, CONNECTICUT

Front Entrance

GAY MANSION, SUFFIELD, CONNECTICUT

prived of the many sources of inspiration which are available in this age of photography and printing, they are to be congratulated on having less distraction. The very limitations of their architectural knowledge made for a fundamental quality of consistency in their works.

A relative limitation which further aided the consistency of builders' and architects' work in the early days of this country lay in the natural limitations of manufacturing mouldings and ornamental detail. Similarity of ideals and the primitive state of mill machinery made for a natural simplicity which today is only the result of conscious study and effort. Today we try to keep our detail simple by referring back to early American work: the early American architect, who was also carpenter and builder, kept his detail simple because he did not know any other kind, and could not have gotten it made if he had known.

Practically every detail was derived from one of the few available books of the time, and these books, for the most part, contained only good and consistent Georgian details. It is interesting to notice in many

HARVEY BISSELL HOUSE — 1815 — SUFFIELD, CONNECTICUT

CHARLES SHEPARD HOUSE — 1824 — SUFFIELD, CONNECTICUT

Porch Detail
HARVEY BISSELL HOUSE,
SUFFIELD, CONNECTICUT

New England towns how successive builders conferred the highest form of flattery upon neighbors and fellow townsmen by imitating some detail which seemed attractive. The treatment of windows in the town of Suffield will be observed from the illustrations to show this imitative tendency. Whether executed by the same builder or by different builders, it is apparent that a good piece of detail was appreciated and duplicated in successive houses.

There were stylistic fads in those days, too, but they differed from our stylistic fads in that they came in waves, and not all at once, as ours do. There was, for instance, the Classic Revival, also called the American Empire, style, which came in after 1812—but the architects, builders, and owners in early American days did not have to worry about Italian villas, French châteaus, English country houses, and California mission houses all at the same time. They concerned themselves only with the thing that was engaging popular fancy at the time, and even more often they concerned themselves only

with immediate local precedent. It is this latter circumstance that makes the old New England village what it is—a page of architectural history rather than a page out of an architectural scrapbook.

Besides the natural similarity in stylistic inspiration in the average New England village, their charming consistency was further aided by a general similarity in building materials, and the difficulty of securing materials alien to the immediate locality.

Several considerations other than its wide availability made white pine one of the most extensively used of early American building materials. The ease with which white pine can be worked, run in mouldings, and carved made it attractive to carpenters, whose tools, in many instances, were few and primitive. No one attribute of white pine, probably, so popularized it with our early builders as its ready workability, for they did know, when they built, that

Porch Detail
CHARLES SHEPARD HOUSE,
SUFFIELD, CONNECTICUT

CAPTAIN TIMOTHY PHELPS HOUSE—1795—SUFFIELD, CONNECTICUT

Entrance Detail
CAPTAIN TIMOTHY PHELPS HOUSE—1795—SUFFIELD, CONNECTICUT

their houses would stand, even without the protection of frequent painting, for hundreds of years.

And, whatever may have been their limitations, they all had the inestimable virtue of simple sincerity. The houses which they built were homes, the foundation of our country today, and their architecture, because it was a sincere effort toward better things, plays its part in our great national architectural heritage, handed down from the first colonists and the first Americans.

THOMAS ARCHER PLACE, SUFFIELD, CONNECTICUT

KENT-HARMON HOUSE, SUFFIELD, CONNECTICUT

EARLY GAMBREL ROOF HOUSE, SUFFIELD, CONNECTICUT

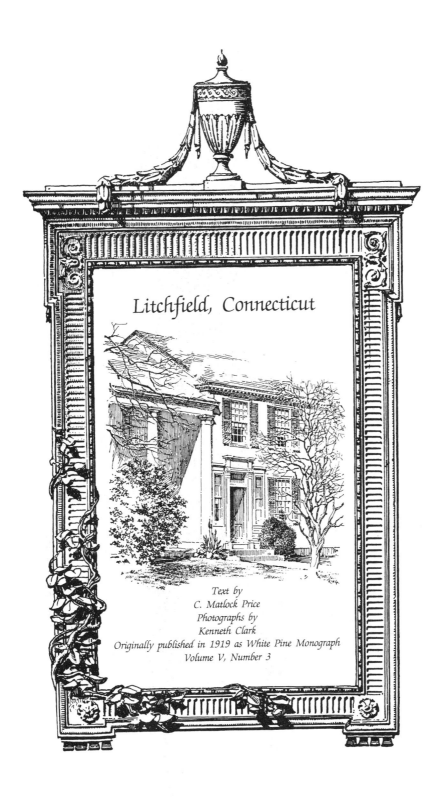

Litchfield, Connecticut

Text by
C. Matlock Price
Photographs by
Kenneth Clark

Originally published in 1919 as White Pine Monograph
Volume V, Number 3

Detail of Entrance and Front Façade
SHELDON HOUSE — 1760 — LITCHFIELD, CONNECTICUT

An interesting minor detail is seen in the device of relating the central projection to the main walls by carrying the entablature of the colonnade over the first story window heads.

HISTORIC HOUSES OF LITCHFIELD

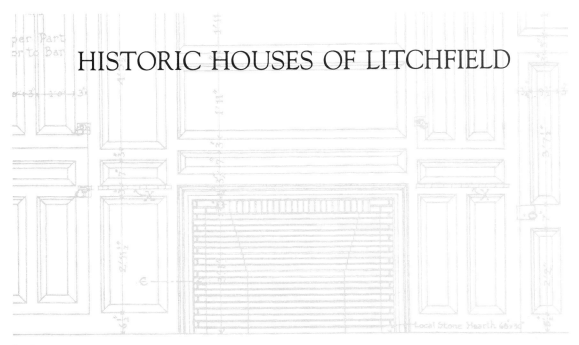

THE poets have said it, and it is true, eternally true—the hill-man turns ever to his hills, and the mariner ever to his seas. And it is with the same instinct that a New Englander turns ever to New England, and finds it as dearly familiar, as much a place of old and known abode as it is essentially different from any other part of the United States.

This one feels with a peculiar intensity on coming back to New England, after some years away. Gray stone walls, old orchards, spreading elms—and always the good, quiet, unpretending houses of other years. The stranger says that New England is austere, even forbidding; but to the New Englander it is ever gentle, ever welcoming. Gray skies, the soft mantle of sea fogs near the coast, the simple oldness and the spirit of quiet and sincere times, these blend themselves, in some way, into a thing that is the spirit of New England.

A typical New England village, founded before the Revolutionary War, and reaching the zenith of its development in 1830 or thereabout, is like no other place in the world. It is a reflection, in contemporary terms, of the lives and ideals of the people who built it; and because of this fact it possesses, in its very essence, qualities of simplicity and sincerity which, today, we find difficult immediately to comprehend or appraise.

There are many such villages scattered through the New England states, from Connecticut to Maine, and many smaller villages, remote from the railroads, sleep beneath their overarching elms, "the world forgetting, by the world forgot."

Although Connecticut is the southernmost of the New England states, its atmosphere is distinctly that of New England, seeming to borrow nothing from adjacent New York State. And so strong (even though undefinable in exact terms) is this "atmosphere" of New England that there is much in common between the seaport towns and the inland towns.

True, the seaport towns have incomparable vistas of blue harbors, and the masts of ships seen at the ends of narrow streets, between silver-gray or white clapboarded houses; yet the same charm, the same spirit that is *only* New England, pervades the old inland villages. Perhaps they are like two tunes composed with the same melody, or two pictures painted with the same range of colors—variations of the same theme.

Among the older inland towns of New England, specifically of Connecticut, one of the most interesting is Litchfield, founded in 1721. The village, as it appeared at the beginning of the next century, would have seemed, to the founders, a splendidly sophisticated place, an eminently satisfying crowning of their first rude endeavors. To realize clearly just what the Litchfield we see today actually means, its pleasant, spacious houses, its serene dignity must be set before a background of the epic simplicity and ruggedness of its pioneer beginnings. And so, a few paragraphs of history, of what is really the epic history of many a similar settlement in New England.

As early as 1715, one John Marsh, a citizen of Hartford, was sent to explore the "Western Lands," as they were called, and he set forth, with a horse and a flintlock musket, through the trails of trappers and hunters. Thus the spot that was to become Litchfield was found—a beautiful spot, with lakes and timber and good farm lands, and a deed of land was duly bought from the Indians for fifteen pounds. Three years later the land was partitioned into holdings for the charter settlers, fifty-five in number, under Deacon John Buel of Lebanon and John Marsh of Hartford, and in 1721 the village was definitely founded and named Litchfield. Possible error of a clerk is supposed to account for

of settlers depended upon scouts ever watchful of the movements of surrounding Indians, whose war dance yells could be heard on the distant hills, while their signal fires gleamed on Mount Tom. In the midst of these perils, and undaunted by their daily hardships and primitive equipment, the founders of Litchfield gradually evolved the beginnings of the peaceful and comfortable village of later years. Their hardships, their toil, their achievements—these are so stimulating to the imagination that one is reluctant

GOVERNOR WOLCOTT HOUSE—1753—SOUTH STREET, LITCHFIELD, CONNECTICUT
The unusual moulding detail of the pediments over the first-story
windows is shown in a special illustration on page 139.

the letter "t," which is not used in the spelling of Lichfield, England, after which the Connecticut village was named.

The pioneers were agriculturists, and the first industries were the gristmill, sawmill and blacksmith shop; the first tradesman, a clothier. The gristmill, it seems, was distinctly a community institution, and while farmers waited for their bags of corn to be ground, they read notices of town meetings posted on the door of the mill, gossiped, traded, and indulged in theological discussions which, if not profound, were at least intense and heated.

For many years the safety of the little group

to turn the page.

The oldest house now standing in Litchfield is the Wolcott House, on South Street, built in 1753 by Oliver Wolcott, one of the signers of the Declaration of Independence, and sometime governor of the state. It was in this house that Mr. Wolcott entertained General Washington and Lafayette.

Architecturally, it represents one of the least pretentious as well as one of the most typical examples of the early New England dwelling. The inland towns and villages of New England being, for the most part, less prosperous than the seaport towns, less elaboration in archi-

TALLMADGE HOUSE, LITCHFIELD, CONNECTICUT
Built in 1775 by Thomas Sheldon.

REEVE-WOODRUFF HOUSE—1773—LITCHFIELD, CONNECTICUT

SEYMOUR HOUSE, LITCHFIELD, CONNECTICUT
Now St. Michael's Rectory

OLD STORE BUILDING—1781—LITCHFIELD, CONNECTICUT
Originally located on North Street. The bowed "show windows" with
the long hood above suggest distinct possibilities for adaptation.

tectural detail is found. Not only were the traders and ship-owners of such towns as Salem and Newport more well-to-do than the struggling settlers who depended upon the land for their livelihood, but in the seaport towns there was available far more talent among artisans. This talent is particularly apparent in such coast towns as Nantucket and the towns on the coast of Maine, as shown in Volume III of this series. Most of the beautiful and often intricate carving and moulding of the old doorways of these towns was the work of skilled carpenters and carvers, who

Detail of South Doorway
HUBBARD HOUSE — 1833 — LITCHFIELD, CONNECTICUT

Detail of Doorway on Corner of North and East Streets
BUTLER HOUSE — 1792 — LITCHFIELD, CONNECTICUT

BUTLER HOUSE—1792—LITCHFIELD, CONNECTICUT

PHELPS HOUSE—1782—LITCHFIELD, CONNECTICUT
The oldest house on East Street.

were enabled, during inclement weather, to spend months of labor upon the embellishment of the better houses.

Fortunately for those of us who would study and admire their craftsmanship, the vigor and often the unstudied genius of their designs, the wood preeminently used by early American builders was seasoned white pine. This wood, often unprotected for years from the hard New England winters, has survived unimpaired. Whether or not they gave thought to its long endurance, it is certain that those early artisans used white pine because of its ready response to the tool, and its adaptability for delicate and elaborate mouldings.

An interesting and unusual moulding detail is seen in the pediments of the first floor windows of the Wolcott House—a mitered break which was a favorite device of early American wood-workers.

Opposite the Wolcott House, on South Street, stands the Reeve-Woodruff House, built in 1773 by Judge Tapping Reeve, who founded here in 1784 the first law school of the United States.

First-Story Window Detail
GOVERNOR WOLCOTT HOUSE—1753—
LITCHFIELD, CONNECTICUT

Entrance Detail
GOVERNOR WOLCOTT HOUSE—1753—
LITCHFIELD, CONNECTICUT

Litchfield has also the distinction of having seen the foundation (and flourishing success) of the first "female seminary" or finishing school for the more advanced education of "young ladies."

A picture of the village of that time enlivens the imagination, and throws something of the glamour of romance over quaint, elm-shaded Litchfield.

"Imagine these now quiet streets, with red coaches rattling through them, with signs of importer, publisher, goldsmith, hatter, etc., hanging on the shops, with young men arriving on horseback to attend the Law School, and divide their attention between their studies of the law and studies of the pretty girls of the 'Female Academy.' Then there were some gay bloods from the South, so much at home in the town that they disported themselves in pink gingham frock coats."

So said an eyewitness. Whether or not the pioneers would have quite approved of the sartorial dandiness of pink frock coats we know not, but it is certain they would have been proud indeed of the distinction which the two

SEYMOUR HOMESTEAD — 1807 — LITCHFIELD, CONNECTICUT

W. H. SANFORD HOUSE — 1832 — LITCHFIELD, CONNECTICUT
Built by Dr. Alanson Abbey.

schools conferred upon Litchfield, making it unquestionably the intellectual and cultural center of the vicinity. Litchfield's paper, the *Monitor*, in 1798, speaks of the Public Library as having existed for some time, and prior to 1831 the "Litchfield Lyceum" conducted lectures, debates and weekly meetings. So, in making the wilderness to bloom, the old pioneers had not wrought in vain with the forces of nature and the malignity of surrounding hostile Indians.

The main streets of Litchfield, broad and elm-shaded, intersect at right angles, but the street names do not carry through the intersection. There are thus, as the arms of the cross, North Street, South Street, East Street and West Street. Along North Street are many of the most interesting of Litchfield's old houses, rich in that expression of very conservative and self-respecting domesticity that characterizes early New England dwellings of their type.

The house said to be the third oldest in the town was built in 1760 by Elisha Sheldon, whose son Samuel made it into the famous Sheldon Tavern or Inn. The central feature of this house, a very agreeably designed Palladian window, above four graceful columns flanking the door, is a distinctly architectural effort, and was repeated, with variation, in the Deming House, directly opposite, across North Street.

Although the old houses of Litchfield are largely of the same type, they show many interesting minor variations, and in many instances some one detail must immediately delight the discerning eye of the architect. Take, for ex-

Entrance Detail
W. H. SANFORD HOUSE—1832—
LITCHFIELD, CONNECTICUT

ample, the very ordinary and uninspiring structure of "Ye Old Curiosity Shoppe" (shown in the picture on page 135)—then discover the brilliant possibilities of adapting the quaint bowed windows with the long hood above them.

To comment, however, upon the current uses which may be made of the details and devices of early American architectural design, is either to embark upon an extensive book, or to discount the intelligence of the architect. The message is rather one for the restless and ill-humored critic who bewails the fact that we have no "native architecture" in this country, and must perforce (or because of a fancied lack of architectural imagination and sanity) borrow European styles. The fact is, that if we borrow European styles, certainly we do so from choice, not from necessity, and certainly not because we lack a distinctive and very flexible national style of our own. In the range from the great Southern plantation manor down to the most diminutive Dutch Colonial farmhouse, there are houses to correspond with every status existing in either the Social Register or Dun's or Bradstreet's.

Perhaps there is an increasing general appreciation of the possibilities and variations to be found in the whole range of early American architecture. By an exact application of the word "Colonial," which is more often used very inexactly, there would exist no designation for the first architecture of the American nation, and all work subsequent to 1776 would either be wrongly named, or would exist without a name.

Entrance Detail

SEYMOUR HOMESTEAD, LITCHFIELD

For this reason, the term "early American," while a little vague for exact definition, should be more generally used than the misapplied term "Colonial," for it embraces not only all pre-Revolutionary work, but also the whole range of American architecture from 1776, through the Classic Revival, which flourished from 1830 until about 1840, or a little later.

"Colonial," too, is inexact because it recognizes no distinction of locality. And certainly there are wide differences between the early buildings of New England and those of the Southern states, not to speak of the locally characteristic styles of Pennsylvania and those parts of New Jersey and New York states which were first settled by the Dutch.

Most important of all the aspects of early American architecture is the consideration of its general spirit, which seems to make itself felt irrespective of locality or of the specific type or style peculiar to a given locality. Yet this spirit is by no means easy to define, for it is made up of several fundamental traits which are nearly always apparent in our earlier buildings. Above all, early American builders built as well as they knew how, both in terms of design and of material. They did not attempt styles which

they did not understand, and they used the most honest and enduring materials available.

Therefore, "style," or "type," did not in the least trouble the builders of Litchfield, and hence the beautiful, unconscious consistency of the place. They were not trying to be clever or ostentatious — they were trying simply to design and build decent, homelike abodes for themselves. As to their success in this — *si monumentum requiris* — there are the illustrations of this chapter, and there is Litchfield itself.

An ancient milestone, just outside the village, gives Litchfield as 102 miles from New York City, by the old King's Highway. Not far, yet we should be glad that old Litchfield is not readily accessible. Such places are easily, very easily spoiled by even a little ill-blended modernity. And they are among the most vital and significant of our national possessions — records and reminders of the lives of dignified aspiration and integrity that built this nation.

Let us reckon this one hundred and two miles from New York by stagecoach (leaving, let us say, Fraunces' Tavern), not by motor car, so that we may keep old Litchfield, serene and unspoiled as it was at the end of last century, in the realm of things "far away and long ago."

Front Door

HUBBARD HOUSE, LITCHFIELD

DEMING HOUSE — 1793 — NORTH STREET, LITCHFIELD, CONNECTICUT

A HOUSE ON NORTH STREET—1785—LITCHFIELD, CONNECTICUT

SANFORD HOUSE—1771—LITCHFIELD, CONNECTICUT

Farmington, Connecticut

Text by
Wesley Sherwood Bessell
Photographs by
Kenneth Clark
Originally published in 1926 as White Pine Monograph
Volume XII, Number 2

Entrance Gateway
ADMIRAL COWLES HOUSE, FARMINGTON, CONNECTICUT

FARMINGTON, CONNECTICUT

FARMINGTON! Why did my thoughts constantly revert to Farmington, what was there to cause such a persistent subconscious recalling of the place? Here I was, thousands of miles away from that village, in a beautiful old town of France—Chartres, in fact, and all day long I had worked on procuring measured drawings of its lovely bits of detail, sketching its architecture and absorbing its past history, wandering through its cathedral and gazing upon its pulpit. By George! that's it, the pulpit, how it all came back to me now, as I lay stretched out upon my bed in a low ceilinged room of the inn where I was sojourning after a full day of joy and of inspiring study, and now dead tired.

I understood clearly now; Chartres, with its centuries old history, its traditions, its beauty and its architecture brought home vividly our own lack of something to show and leave to the world. I could not help thinking of how ridiculous it would be to travel the distance I had, and to register at an hotel in Passaic, New Jersey, or Nyack, New York, or Lansing, Michigan, in order that I might study our own architecture and make measured drawings of its mouldings and become enthralled by it all.

Then my mind reverted again to Farmington and the few years I lived there, and really after all, there were places one could kick up an interest in, but how few and how meager and small the number of examples in such communities. Still there was Farmington, it had probably more to show than the average.

Oh yes, that's it, that pulpit in the old church, I must be drowsy after my day, in fact I must have fallen asleep, for I was sitting stiff backed in one of the pews of the old church, the church upon completion of which the builder was paid partly by a hogshead of rum. Shades of Volstead, think of it, yes sir, it was the old minister delivering his sermon, pounding now upon the rail of that pulpit with its beautiful old Colonial detail; through the circular-headed window the warm spring sun streamed into the church, the windows were open and one could hear the song of happy young birds. Old Abigail Potter made that pulpit, and what a wonderful bit of work it was, he loved it, was proud of it, and had

enjoyed the work of doing it. I must stand up, the old minister is through, wonder what he said? That pulpit certainly diverted my mind from the sermon. Oh there, going out now, what a delightful day, there is old Captain Gibbons, he is working on that new canal that is going to connect Farmington with New Haven. Must be discussing it with his friends. He lives in the house on Farmington Avenue. Oh yes, he's just had an old knocker made of brass and lettered with his name for the front door, he needs it too, I spent many moments trying to make him hear my knock on the door, getting sore knuckles for my efforts.

Guess I must start meandering down the road a bit, been invited to dinner at the Cowles'. My how Abigail loves to surprise us, just look at that door to the Deming House, has pilaster caps, all of his own conception, but what a lovely solid paneled door, hope no one ever destroys it, the whole door is rather exceptional, but then doorways are so alluring to work on. Just look at that one of Gay's, the paneling almost like the Deming's, but entirely different, and then the door on Obadiah Alcorn's without a cap, what a lovely fence too. The cornice also is interesting, remember how they struggled over the bracket at the corner, don't think there is another like it.

Up through the trees on the upper street, I see the old Whitman House with that overhanging second floor; we have only an Indian here and there now, but a few years back they used to shoot Indians through a hole from the second floor in that overhang, but I must be getting along, the old town is full of those bits of Colonial details, cornices, doorways, rainwater heads, and I must make some sketches here some day. There is the house of General Cowles with two curious features, the front door with its inverted columns and the side porch with its five columns and pediment. How that center column seems to hold up the Palladian window in the pediment, and what a thin amount of masonry over those arches at the porch floor level. Still, the whole thing looks well, and quite like Charleston. It's a stranger in our northern village, but very welcome.

And now I am at the gate of Admiral Cowles' residence where I am to dine. No gate quite like this one, you know, the house was the product of a young English Army officer while stationed over here during the Revolution, who must have been an architect in England, drafted into the service. He left his imprint by way of the Cowles' House; he must have been in India too, see the swastika worked into the gate. I knock at the front door and am admitted, it's a lovely bit of atmosphere that greets me; how hungry I am, and how I shall enjoy eating in such surroundings. Food tastes so different, doesn't it, in a pure white Colonial room with paneled walls and beautiful doors, and a lovely detailed cornice?

Yes sir, that was a meal, and I am about to depart, the front door is open, and that gate through the front door, is it not a picture?

Well, as I step toward this sunlight, the picture begins to fade, I feel a sense of impending danger, things begin to look dark, I am hungry, ah, I know, I was dreaming. I am in France at Chartres, but, I am also still hungry, hungry for a return of our delightful old village, thousands of miles is a long way to travel for inspiration; it ought to be near at home. Well there are a few villages offering their wealth, and of these few still left, one is Farmington.

The Gateway Seen Through the Front Door
ADMIRAL COWLES HOUSE, FARMINGTON, CONNECTICUT

WHITMAN HOUSE, FARMINGTON, CONNECTICUT

Detail of Entrance Doorway
DEMING HOUSE, FARMINGTON, CONNECTICUT

Detail of Bracket and Drop
"OLDER" COWLES HOUSE — 1661 — FARMINGTON, CONNECTICUT

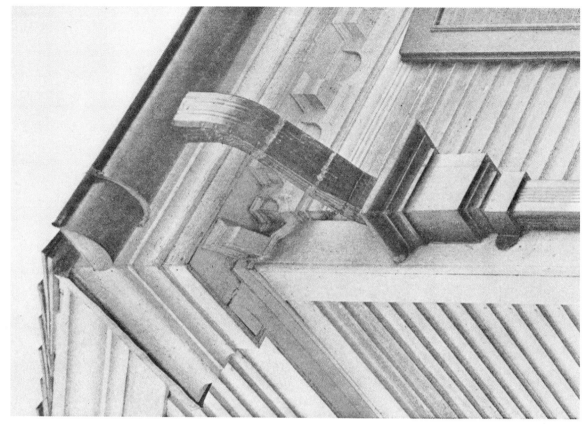

OBADIAH ALCORN HOUSE

ADMIRAL COWLES HOUSE

CORNICE AND LEADER HEAD DETAILS—FARMINGTON, CONNECTICUT

Cornice and Leader Head Detail
HOUSE AT FARMINGTON, CONNECTICUT

Entrance Doorway
OBADIAH ALCORN HOUSE, FARMINGTON, CONNECTICUT

Mantelpiece Side of the West Parlor
COWLES-LEWIS HOUSE, FARMINGTON, CONNECTICUT

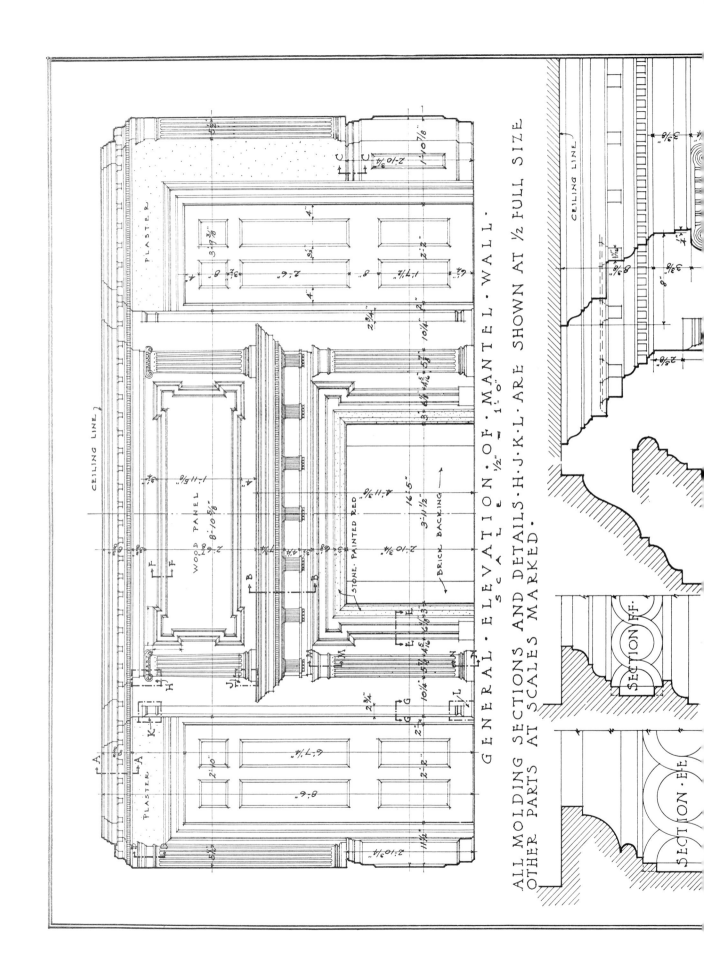

GENERAL · ELEVATION · OF · MANTEL · WALL ·
SCALE ½" = 1'·0"

ALL MOLDING SECTIONS AND DETAILS · H · J · K · L · ARE SHOWN AT ½ FULL SIZE
OTHER PARTS AT SCALES MARKED.

CEILING LINE

PLASTER

WOOD PANEL

STONE · PAINTED RED

BRICK BACKING

CEILING LINE

SECTION · F·F·

SECTION · E·E·

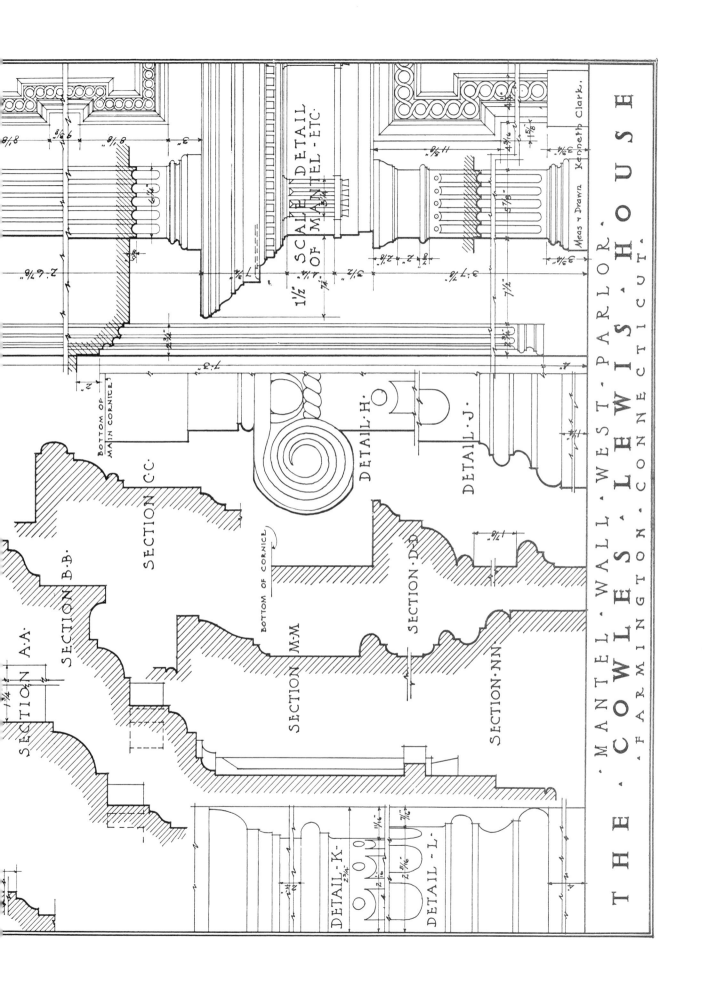

SCALE DETAIL OF MANTEL · ETC·

1½" SCALE DETAIL

Meas & Drawn Kenneth Clark.

BOTTOM OF MAIN CORNICE·

BOTTOM OF CORNICE

SECTION ·C·C·

SECTION ·B·B·

SECTION ·A·A·

SECTION ·M·M·

SECTION ·D·D·

SECTION·NN·

DETAIL·H·

DETAIL·J·

DETAIL·K·

DETAIL·L·

· THE · COWLES · HOUSE ·
· MANTEL · WALL · WEST · PARLOR ·
· FARMINGTON · CONNECTICUT ·

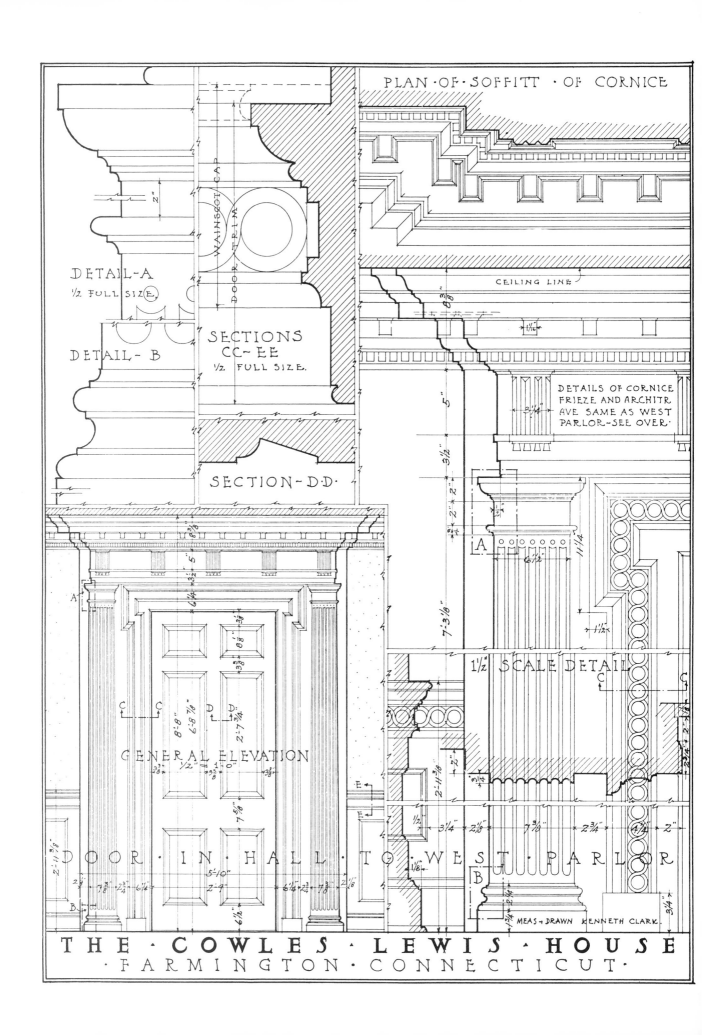

PLAN·OF·SOFFITT·OF CORNICE

CEILING LINE

DETAIL-A
½ FULL SIZE

DETAIL - B

WAINSCOT CAP

DOOR TRIM

SECTIONS
CC- EE
½ FULL SIZE.

DETAILS OF CORNICE
FRIEZE AND ARCHITR
AVE SAME AS WEST
PARLOR-SEE OVER·

SECTION~D·D·

1½ SCALE DETAIL

GENERAL ELEVATION

DOOR · IN · HALL · TO · WEST · PARLOR

MEAS + DRAWN   KENNETH CLARK.

THE · COWLES · LEWIS · HOUSE
· FARMINGTON · CONNECTICUT ·

Hall Doorway
COWLES-LEWIS HOUSE, FARMINGTON, CONNECTICUT

Bedroom Mantel

Looking Into the Dining Room

COWLES-LEWIS HOUSE, FARMINGTON, CONNECTICUT

ADMIRAL COWLES HOUSE, FARMINGTON, CONNECTICUT

PORTER HOUSE, FARMINGTON, CONNECTICUT

Side Porch
GENERAL COWLES HOUSE, FARMINGTON, CONNECTICUT

Detail of Pendant
WHITMAN HOUSE, FARMINGTON, CONNECTICUT

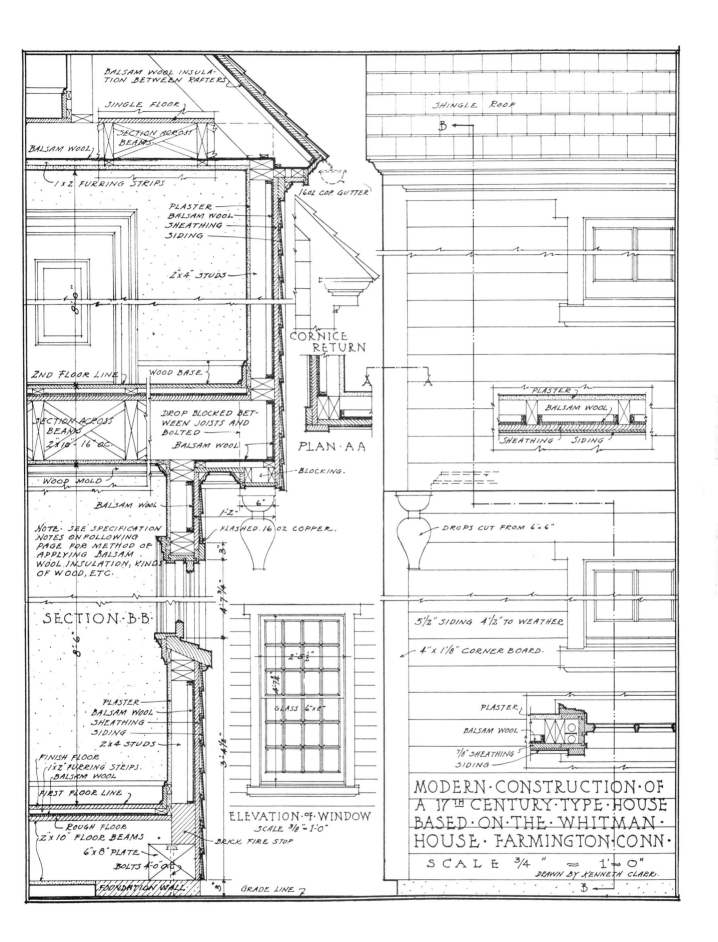

BALSAM WOOL INSULATION BETWEEN RAFTERS

SINGLE FLOOR

SECTION ACROSS BEAMS

BALSAM WOOL

1 x 2 FURRING STRIPS

PLASTER
BALSAM WOOL
SHEATHING
SIDING

2"x 4" STUDS

2ND FLOOR LINE

WOOD BASE

SECTION ACROSS BEAMS 2"x10"-16" O.C.

DROP BLOCKED BETWEEN JOISTS AND BOLTED

BALSAM WOOL

WOOD MOLD

BALSAM WOOL

NOTE· SEE SPECIFICATION NOTES ON FOLLOWING PAGE FOR METHOD OF APPLYING BALSAM WOOL INSULATION, KINDS OF WOOD, ETC.

1'-2"

6"

FLASHED.16 OZ COPPER.

SECTION·B·B·

8'-6"

PLASTER
BALSAM WOOL
SHEATHING
SIDING
2"x 4" STUDS

FINISH FLOOR
1"x 2" FURRING STRIPS.
BALSAM WOOL

FIRST FLOOR LINE

ROUGH FLOOR
2"x 10" FLOOR BEAMS
6"x 8" PLATE
BOLTS 4'-0" O.C.

BRICK FIRE STOP

FOUNDATION WALL

16 OZ. COP. GUTTER

CORNICE RETURN

BLOCKING.

PLAN·AA

ELEVATION·OF·WINDOW
SCALE 3/8" = 1'-0"

2'-6½"
4'-7⅞"
GLASS 6"x 8"

3'-4½"

4'-7¾"

3"

GRADE LINE

SHINGLE ROOF

B

A   A

PLASTER
BALSAM WOOL
SHEATHING   SIDING

DROPS CUT FROM 6"x 6"

5½" SIDING 4½" TO WEATHER

4"x 1⅛" CORNER BOARD.

PLASTER
BALSAM WOOL
⅞" SHEATHING
SIDING

MODERN·CONSTRUCTION·OF
A 17ᵀᴴ CENTURY·TYPE·HOUSE
BASED·ON·THE·WHITMAN·
HOUSE·FARMINGTON·CONN·
SCALE 3/4 " = 1'-0"
DRAWN BY KENNETH CLARK·

B

Detail of Doorway
GENERAL COWLES HOUSE, FARMINGTON, CONNECTICUT

Essex: A Connecticut
River Town

Text by
H. Van Buren Magonigle
Photographs by
Kenneth Clark
Originally published in 1920 as White Pine Monograph
Volume VI, Number 6

OLD HOUSE AT RIVER END OF LITTLE POINT STREET, ESSEX, CONNECTICUT

ESSEX:
A CONNECTICUT RIVER TOWN

"I remember the black wharves and the slips
  And the sea tides tossing free:
And the Spanish sailors with bearded lips.
And the beauty and mystery of the ships
  And the magic of the sea."

THERE are no black wharves now if ever there were, nor slips, and the sea tides barely reach it; the last Spanish whiskerado who swaggered through her streets has long since been gathered, beard and all, to his fathers—but as by the perfume of a memory Essex is haunted still by "the beauty and mystery of the ships and the magic of the sea." Dreaming by the river, the drone of the motors on the state highway further back does not disturb her peace. Her dreams are of that earlier day when the first Lays and Haydens came to Potapaug Point and Uriah Hayden built the old Ship Tavern just where the road which is now Essex Main Street came down to the river and the ferry to Ely's Landing on the easterly bank, nearly opposite. It is said that in Massachusetts the county of Suffolk lies north of Norfolk county; this seems so much too good to be true that I never investigated the

VILLAGE SMITHY, ESSEX, CONNECTICUT

authenticity of the report. It is for the same reason that I decline to inquire why Essex is on the west bank of the river. There was a busy intercourse between the two banks, for in the old days the ferry at Old Lyme and the Essex-Ely's Landing Ferry seem to have been the only regular means of crossing the river between its lower reaches and Hartford. There is a legend that Daniel Webster, on his way from Boston to Washington, reaching the river after the ice had stopped the ferry service and before it was strong enough to bear the weight of a traveling coach, spent several days on the easterly bank in the hope of a freeze and finally had to drive up to Hartford and cross there—a tale which throws interesting light upon the leisurely pace and delightful inconvenience of travel in the youth of this Republic.

It was on Potapaug or Big Point that the old shipyards were (they were burnt by the British in

1812)—on the north side of Essex Main Street. The Lays seem to have been the first owners of the whole point and the Haydens to have bought from them the land on the southerly side. But Haydens and Pratts and Lays intermarried as people will and it is difficult now and quite unprofitable for a stranger to attempt to unravel the rival claims to priority and prestige which the inquiries in even a few hours' sojourn stir up. These Lays and Haydens were all shipbuilders and shipmasters; as a measure of the town's traditions, out of eight male Haydens in one family seven were sea captains. In those days the two bridges down at Old Lyme were not dreamed of— now they seem to be a barrier between Essex and that sea with which she had then so close a tie

JOHN PRATT HOUSE, MAIN STREET, ESSEX, CONNECTICUT

and of which the river mouth was a gateway, the Sound but a vestibule. Not a vestige remains of the old yards where they built the tall clipper ships for the China trade and vessels of lesser tonnage for coastwise traffic; but on a quiet autumn day one has but to close one's eyes to hear the ring of the mallets and to smell the oakum and the tar that stopped the seams of those gallant craft—ships which linked a little village in Connecticut to the Flowery Kingdom and all the fragrant East. It is a haven now for the old cup-defender *Dauntless*, and it was on a quest for her that we made a detour from the high road and first found Essex. Moving swiftly through the streets I received an impression of many curved roofs covering low, snug houses, and I was prepared to

LONG YELLOW HOUSE, WEST AVENUE, ESSEX, CONNECTICUT

Detail of Side Elevation
OLD SHIP TAVERN, ESSEX, CONNECTICUT

Detail of River Side
OLD SHIP TAVERN, ESSEX, CONNECTICUT

account for them by Dutch influence. But not a Dutchman nor a Dutch name was to be found on a second visit, only good old British names like the Lays, the Haydens, the Pratts, the Lewises, Starkeys and Hinghams. Nor could I find more than three curved roofs in the entire town; but for these it is easy to account— one at least was built by a ship-builder, another by a sea captain of a type more sensitive to influences than the rest and who wished to recall ashore the sweep of line of his home afloat. At all events I am prepared to maintain that in an atmosphere of New England primness these sweeping roof lines are as refreshing as a breath of the sea— a primness which must have been somewhat mitigated at times if we may trust the mute witness of a bill of sale to Molly Lay, hung up in the old Ship Tavern, and of which the chief items are rum and gin.

The old Hayden Homestead, the third house up from the river on Essex Main Street, has a hip roof, unusual among its gabled neighbors. It seems that up the river at Windsor "they knew how to make such roofs," and there was a carpenter of parts who knew the secrets of cutting rafter bevels and such, and instead of traveling about to do the work stayed comfortably at home and shipped the shaped lumber. The roof framing, at least, of this house and possibly the whole frame, was rafted down the river

Entrance Porch

PARKER HOMESTEAD, ESSEX, CONNECTICUT

and one other roof in the village is reputed to have made a similar voyage. There is every evidence of a quiet prosperity in the character of the exterior detail of many of the houses, although, except in the Tavern, the interiors are quite without interest; not even first-rate chimney-pieces survive. And the town as a whole has suffered from the Greek Revival—a Greek with a particularly heavy hand appears to have been resuscitated.

Coming up the river or along the state highway between Saybrook and Hartford, you may see Essex— the new Essex— climbing her hill among the trees. And dwellers in the old Essex and the new climb of a Sunday to the four churches whose spires and towers of the most fearful and wonderful design prick through the leafy screen, ugly but picturesque. Around these churches, set quite close together in a neighborly way, quite in contrast with the usual superior airs of withdrawal and isolation churches of differing tenets seem to give themselves, are interesting arrangements of shady levels and of roads ramping up and roads ramping down, altogether distinctive in the atmosphere they create. From this upper level, West Avenue leads over and down to the state road. "Avenue" has a suspiciously modern sound—and in spite of one or two good old things like the Parker Homestead and one little, old, long yellow house, has little of interest to commend it except the Village Smithy,

OLD STARKEY PLACE, MAIN STREET, ESSEX, CONNECTICUT

27 MAIN STREET, ESSEX, CONNECTICUT

OLD TOWN HALL ON THE HILL, ESSEX, CONNECTICUT

TWO HOUSES ON ESSEX MAIN STREET

in which the fifth generation of Pratts, a family of seamen and smiths, still follows one of the family callings. The location of the smithy would seem to indicate the importance of this road (or Avenue, as it seems to prefer being called) as the principal connecting link between the river and the high road in days gone by. But although the old Town Hall is well up on the flank of this hill, it is the very oldest part down by the river which means Essex—Essex Main Street, the

t' die"—an opinion he would not wish me to share.

However ardent an advocate of progress one may be in theory, it is in towns like this that one regrets its march. Instead of the old coaches lumbering down to the ferry with all the picturesque accompaniments of a stop and a drop at the Tavern, an occasional copy of the works of Mr. Henry Ford (himself, it will be remembered, an advocate of peace and the supercargo

COLONEL LEWIS HOUSE, MAIN STREET, ESSEX, CONNECTICUT

street next to it called with blunt simplicity Back Street, Little Point Street, where the old George Hayden House stands and where, opposite, running down toward the river, are three or four tiny, low, one-story cottages, which, taken together, give a very definite charm and character to the street. One of them was built by Uncle Noah Tucker, and Cap'n Charley Hayden has lived in it for forty-two years; he and his brother George in the street adjoining are the last survivors of the Hayden family. Cap'n Charley declares them to be "t' old and t' ugly

of a peace ship), rattles and coughs, shakes with its peculiar palsy and invades the brooding peace of the waterside. Instead of the old shipping of Revolutionary times, trim motor launches and smart small sailing craft mark the difference between sailing as a pastime and sailing as a life to be lived. But as the shadows grow longer and the reaches of the beautiful river begin to draw to themselves the cobweb texture of the twilight, the ghosts of old ships ride on the rising tide and Essex, dreaming still, comes into her own again. It is only in dreams we find our own.

ONE OF THE OLD HOUSES ON LITTLE POINT STREET
ESSEX, CONNECTICUT

OLD STARKEY PLACE, MAIN STREET
ESSEX, CONNECTICUT

COLONEL LEWIS HOUSE

HOUSE OPPOSITE ST. JOHN'S CHURCH

TWO DOORWAYS ON MAIN STREET, ESSEX, CONNECTICUT

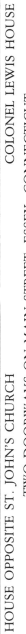

PRATT HOUSE, BACK STREET, ESSEX, CONNECTICUT

River Towns of Connecticut

Text by
William D. Foster
Photographs by
Kenneth Clark
Originally published in 1923 as White Pine Monograph
Volume XI, Number 2

HOUSE AT WINDSOR, CONNECTICUT
Windsor, with Hartford and Wethersfield, formed the famous early
River Towns of the Connecticut Valley.

THE RIVER TOWNS OF CONNECTICUT

IN the early days of the Massachusetts Colony, there were a number of the colonists who felt that the district around Boston was becoming too thickly settled for them, as well as that the religious and political attitude of their neighbors was too strict, and accordingly, with what possessions they could manage, little groups set off westward into the unexplored wilderness, without any idea of their destination and with no knowledge of the country, other than various tales of the Indians to be found there. Eventually, these courageous explorers reached the Connecticut River, and there, where the valley invited settlement, not only with water and meadows, but also with exposure to the sun and a pleasant climate afforded by its north and south direction they founded a straggling line of towns, which extended for nearly a hundred miles in length.

Among these towns were Windsor, Hartford and Wethersfield, the so-called River Towns of Connecticut. The other groups of settlements in Connecticut were those around New Haven and those of New London. The River Towns, however, were the earliest, Hartford having been settled in 1636 by Hooker and his group of one hundred emigrants from Cambridge, while Windsor and Wethersfield were established by others from Watertown and Dorchester.

These settlers underwent great struggles for existence during the first years in their new homes; the Indians, who were friendly at first, soon took to the war path and an almost interminable struggle began. It was also a long way to their base of supplies, a trip by boat around Cape Cod, through the Sound and then up the river, a trip that was fraught with hazards. Accordingly, the first houses that were built, after the period of simple abris which served as preliminary shelters, were quite simple and somewhat crude. The plans were generally of one or two rooms on each floor with a central chimney, and the entry and stairs in the space in front of this. The next step in planning was the lean-to which provided a kitchen and bedroom, but during the last quarter of the century, this became not only a usual part of the house, but part of the original plan. The lean-to was pretty generally abandoned for the full two stories during the early eighteenth century, and with the increased depth of the house, the simple gable roof was frequently changed to a gambrel, and the long slope over the lean-to ceased to exist.

During this time, when the typical plan was changing, materials were becoming more plentiful, and undoubtedly the process of building was becoming more familiar, so that larger and more substantial houses were being erected; small "estates" were being established along the broad streets of the towns, the houses at the road, with meadows and farm land extending back in the valley to the foothills. With this increasing comfort and security more attention began to be paid to the ornamental features of the houses, to the doorways, the window trims, and the cornices, which were executed more or less crudely from the memory of the English work the builders had seen.

It is generally with the houses of this period that the interest in Colonial architecture as prototypes for present day work begins, and I sometimes think it would be fortunate for modern domestic architecture if our interest had ceased with that period. The widely distributed general familiarity with the later and more ornate forms have lead to the achievement of much "Colonial" work today which is only a collection of tricks, with small scale detail generously distributed, making fussy compositions, regardless of the authenticity of the various elements. To study these eighteenth century houses with their simple masses and their decorative features well placed, though frequently crude, is a pleasure, and gives one a sense of the solidity and virility that is essential in real architecture, a sense that even the most untutored layman unconsciously feels and which makes him admire and desire the

Detail of Doorway
HOUSE AT WINDSOR, CONNECTICUT

old houses of New England. The houses illustrated in this chapter are all of the general eighteenth century period. They are typical of the River Towns and of the Massachusetts part of the valley, and yet they are also typical of the other Connecticut settlements. The other groups, New Haven and New London, did not vary greatly in their political forms from the River Towns, and neither did they vary greatly in their use of architectural forms. There was the same general plan; the differences were differences of detail.

The house at Windsor, which is shown on page 182, is one of the unusual examples where the gable end faces the street, so that practically all of the decorative effect is on this one façade which gives almost a public character to the building. It is one of the later houses, and the detail has become quite accurate, though not over-elaborate. The fence is particularly good in design, adding a great deal to the charm of the composition and becoming an essential part of the design, when the house stands so near the street.

The Webb House in Wethersfield is undoubt-

Detail of Doorway
WEBB HOUSE, WETHERSFIELD, CONNECTICUT

WEBB HOUSE, WETHERSFIELD, CONNECTICUT

HOUSE AT ROCKY HILL, CONNECTICUT

HOUSE AT WINDSOR, CONNECTICUT

TWO OF THE TYPES OF DOORWAYS FOUND IN RIVER TOWNS

WAREHAM WILLIAMS HOUSE, NORTHFORD, CONNECTICUT

HOUSE AT WINDSOR, CONNECTICUT

TWO OF THE TYPES OF DOORWAYS FOUND IN RIVER TOWNS

WAREHAM WILLIAMS HOUSE, NORTHFORD, CONNECTICUT

OLIVER ELLSWORTH HOUSE, WINDSOR, CONNECTICUT

edly the best known in that locality, not only because of its architectural qualities, but also because of the national historical interest which it bears. It was there, during the time when it was Joseph Webb's Tavern, that Washington and Rochambeau held a council and decided on the plans for the Yorktown campaign. Obscured by the trees in our photograph is an ell which extends behind the main portion of the house and at right angles to it; this was the original early house, with a second story overhang it was moved back from the street in 1750 to allow the larger house to be built. The façade is very well proportioned, and has excellent fenestration; the large windows, with their twenty-four panes, giving remarkable dignity. While the porch, as it exists, may be later, it undoubtedly replaced one of practically the same design and proportion.

In construction, the Webb House has a certain archaeological interest as it marks the transition in this district from the early to the later method of framing for the floor joists. The left hand portion has the early method where the "summer" runs parallel with the ridge, while the other half of the house, though certainly built at the same time, has the later method of running the "summer" from the header at the chimney to the front wall, parallel with the end walls. The Wareham Williams House in Northford is of the same general type again, but the doorway places it as earlier than the Webb House. This doorway, with the

WATSON HOUSE, EAST WINDSOR HILL

one at Windsor, shown on page 187, and the doorway from the Silas Deane House at Wethersfield, shown on page 194, are quite typical of the Connecticut Valley work for the first half of the Eighteenth century. They show clearly that the precedent for applied features was English; the general forms are distinctly English, adapted to wood, while the mouldings follow the classic, that is, the classic as debased in the English Renaissance, as nearly as memory and the tools at hand would permit. Crude though they may be, they possess a fine vigor and a sense of scale which is usually appropriate.

Judging from the differences in window trim, it would seem that the Oliver Ellsworth House, at Windsor, is one of the typical houses which was later enlarged. The two chimneys mark the ends of the original house, a well-proportioned façade not unlike many others, but with the addition of the two storied porch, and the lengthening of the house, it takes on much of the character of the Litchfield houses, and is rather unique for the River Towns district.

The three-story houses which were built in Salem and Providence between 1780 and 1820 are not found much in Connecticut and the Watson House at Windsor Locks is one of the few that were built. The doorway shows a great deal more sophistication and finesse than the earlier work, while the Ionic caps and the Palladian motive over the doorway bespeak a greater knowledge of details and a greater effort at design than is shown in the simpler houses. In the Old Inn on the Hartford Road we see the same attempt to achieve an architectural effect.

The long first-story windows in the house at Windsor Hill, shown on page 193, rather mar the Colonial feeling of an otherwise pleasing elevation. Almost mid-Victorian in their proportion, it is probable that they were enlarged sometime after the original construction. The doorway is extremely interesting, and very much like those on the Stebbins House in Deerfield; the small arched, Palladian-like panes in the transom have a decided Georgian feeling, and form another link in this close relationship between the architecture of the two countries.

In the farmhouse at Rocky Hill, once part of Wethersfield, we find the overhang at the second floor on the front, while on the gable end it occurs at both the second and third stories. This slight overhang was used on many of the houses of the early part of the century, and is all that remains of the greater projections which occur on the seventeenth century houses, where they were frequently ornamented with large carved drops. What the origin of the overhang was, is a question that has been much discussed. Some writers have maintained that the large early projections were to afford space for loopholes through which the occupants could offer resistance to attacking parties of Indians or other enemies. This premise, on the face of it, seems somewhat absurd,

OLD INN, HARTFORD ROAD, CONNECTICUT

as the protection afforded would be against only those who had reached the walls of the house.

The most reasonable supposition for the unusual framing would be that the carpenter-architects were using the English methods with which they were familiar. That is, in certain parts of the west of England, there are various examples of timber construction where the overhangs were formed by cutting large pieces of timber down to the size of the corner posts for the first story, and the upper end left larger, forming the projection to carry the posts above. In many cases this was then repeated for the next story as well. In the case of the English work, where the surfaces of this type of construction were generally covered with stucco, these overhangs served the purpose of protecting the walls below from the weather; they also afforded on the upper floors a little more space than was permitted on the street floors. From the fact that we know that certain of the settlers of Connecticut came from the parts of England and that some of the same group were around Ipswich, where the second story overhangs also occur very frequently, it seems quite logical to assume that they were simply following the methods with which they were most familiar.

On our Colonial houses the overhangs were only decorative and were gradually reduced until the projection was only a few inches, or room for a series of mouldings, as seen in this example at

Rocky Hill. The doorway here has been worked into the projection very knowingly, the mouldings lining up with the bed molds of the cornice; but in the case of the doorway at Windsor, shown on page 186, the builder naively solved his problem simply by breaking out the trim at the overhang, rather than by trying for an architectural solution.

The difference between the houses of the first part of the eighteenth century and the latter part was largely due to the Revolution, and its effects on the general population. Just as in the case of the Great War, building in general was pretty much at a standstill during the Revolution, and afterwards it was found that, while many persons had lost their money, others had accumulated fortunes from the industries that were built up by the war. And so we find that more pretentious houses were demanded. With this general activity came the publication of books, both in England and in America, concerning architectural forms and details, chief among them being Asher Benjamin's *Country Builder's Assistant*, published at Greenfield in 1797. These books gave

Detail of Doorway
HOUSE AT WINDSOR HILL, CONNECTICUT

more accurate details of the Classic and Renaissance periods and actually started the study of architecture in this country. Accordingly, architects appeared whose individuality marked their work from that of others, bringing their names with their designs down to the present time.

The study of the Classic forms soon started the Greek Revival, the next step in our architectural development, which, in turn, was followed by the Queen Anne cottages and the Victorian era of bad taste. Organized architectural education, both here and abroad freed us somewhat from these "Styles," took us through the French influence of the 1890's and brought us to the present period of such complete information that today we are able to design in any style the client may request with more or less success.

However, through all this confusion, there still persists a very genuine interest and appreciation of our first American architectural period and for the architect who would achieve the restful simplicity of the work of the truly Colonial times, the simple, well-proportioned houses of the eighteenth century will continue to be an inspiration and delight.

Detail of Doorway
FARMHOUSE, ROCKY HILL, CONNECTICUT

FARMHOUSE, ROCKY HILL, CONNECTICUT

HOUSE AT WINDSOR HILL, CONNECTICUT

Detail of Doorway
SILAS DEANE HOUSE, WETHERSFIELD, CONNECTICUT

Old Hill Towns of
Windham County,
Connecticut

Text by
Richard H. Dana, Jr.
Photographs by
Kenneth Clark
Originally published in 1924 as White Pine Monograph
Volume X, Number 1

Detail of Portico
PERKINS HOUSE — 1832 — WINDHAM, CONNECTICUT

THE OLD HILL TOWNS OF WINDHAM COUNTY, CONNECTICUT

THE early settlers in the northeast corner of Connecticut — Windham County — located their towns on the hilltops to secure greater safety from the Indians. They planned more wisely than they knew; for not only were their towns preserved from destruction by the Indians in the late seventeenth century, but also from destruction by industrialism and Victorian prosperity in the late nineteenth century. And, fortunately, the twentieth century knows enough to value and preserve them!

The first period in the history of these towns was a tale, many times retold, of hardship, struggle and endurance. The region was known as early as 1635, as it was on the direct route from the Massachusetts Bay Colony to the Connecticut River Settlements. This "hideous and trackless wilderness" was traversed by only the roughest sort of trail, known as the Connecticut Path. The first definite settlement of any kind within the county area was made in 1686, by thirty courageous families from Roxbury, Massachusetts, who toiled along the eighty miles of wild country to form a new community at "New Roxbury," which later became known as Woodstock. Settlers in other parts of the county came from Norwich, Connecticut, which lay several miles to the south of the present county line. All had the same trying experience. Land purchases from the Indians were most uncertain. The English governor of the Connecticut colony added to this uncertainty by trying to appropriate all these purchases to the Crown, saying that the signature of an Indian was not worth more than

a scratch of a bear's paw. The French and Indian War still further delayed settlements everywhere. Then came the clearing of the ground, building the houses and barns, disputes about boundaries and the difficult task of establishing a minister and raising a church in each remote settlement. However, before 1775 all this was fairly accomplished almost everywhere in the county.

The second period, after the Revolution, was one of great prosperity throughout the county. Stagecoach roads were built up to these towns, no matter how steep or high or rough the hill. They were no longer isolated and remote. They were connected by high roads to Hartford, Providence, Norwich and the towns in Massachusetts. Stagecoach inns were opened and flourished in each town. Three of these inns are now open and still offer their hospitality all the year around; the Ben Grosvenor Inn at Pomfret, the Chelsea Inn at Hampton Hill and the Windham Inn at Windham. Their decorative old sign boards are still swinging in the breeze.

The third period came with the railroads and the building of factories in the last half of the nineteenth century. The railroad naturally followed the rivers and valleys and several modern manufacturing towns sprang up along the Natchaug and Quinebaug Rivers. The old stagecoach lines were discontinued and the commerce with the outside world lapsed; so that the old hill towns again found themselves left high and dry. But, though this may have been a disappointment to a few ambitious merchants in these towns, it proved to be a blessing in disguise. Well removed from the nearest railroad, they are preserved today as delightful residential villages, with all the charm and atmosphere of a hundred years ago.

Canterbury is the most appealing of the sixteen old towns in Windham County. It was considered important enough architecturally to have devoted to it Chapter 14 of this volume.

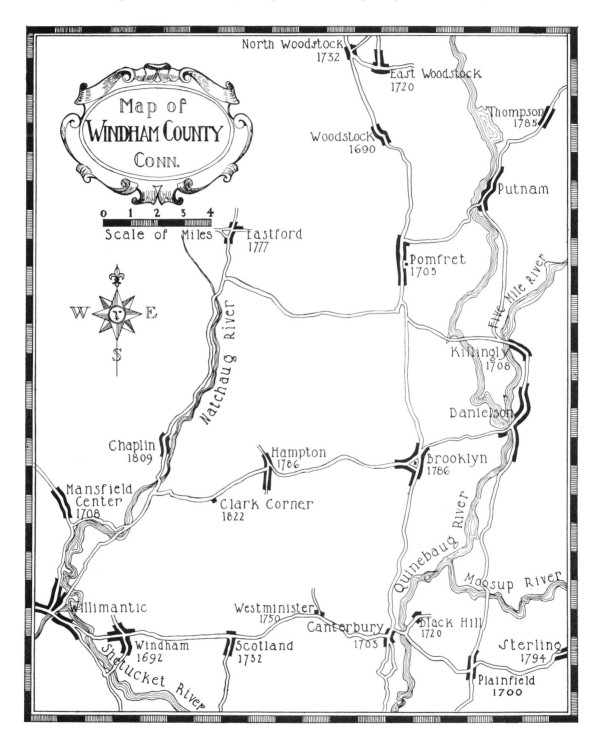

WINDHAM was settled in 1689 by sixteen gentlemen from Norwich. Its unusual advantages and proximity to Norwich attracted a superior class of citizens, men of character, position and public spirit. Windham Green soon increased in business and importance. Here were town clerk, constable, justices and leading men. There was much good fellowship among early settlers, feasting, merrymaking and interchange of hospitalities. The young people remained at home, marry-

By 1750 social life was noted as exceedingly "hilarious and enjoyable"; "jaunting and junketing" were popular. Windham people were especially noted for their love of fun and frolic, bantering and jesting others. One joke was turned on them, however. Fear of the French and the Indians was still persisting, when on a very dark, sultry summer night, a roar and tumult filled the town. The people, perplexed and greatly frightened, stayed behind barred doors and listened

WEBB HOUSE, WINDHAM, CONNECTICUT

ing mostly among their own townspeople, till, in the process of years, the whole population was knit together in one great family circle. In 1726 Windham was made shire town of the county. Though far to the southwest of the center of the county, no one thought of disputing her claim. She had far outstripped her sister townships in population, wealth, cultivation and political influence. The first court of the county was held at Windham Green and soon after a court house and jail were erected.

with horror, no one venturing out to face the foe. Next morning it was discovered that it was only a migration through the town of noisy bullfrogs in search of water, their own pond having dried up. Much to the mortification of the Windham people the story flew all over the county and the country.

Just south of the Green stands the old Webb House, which was built during the early days of Windham's settlement. The house has an unusual L-shaped plan, with two long fronts of equal

Side Door
WEBB HOUSE, WINDHAM, CONNECTICUT

ture which flourished in the United States during the period of the Classic Revival. The house as well as the portico has a broad pediment. The front is faced with tongued and grooved siding put on vertically, giving a flat serene background and forming a pleasing contrast to the fluted columns of the front portico. There are two chimneys on each end with the side walls between them covered with clapboards. The wing at the side is also clapboarded. The Ionic portico (page 196) is so consummately well proportioned that we are not surprised to find that the designer gave special study to the most advantageous manner of spacing the columns, to further the design as a whole. It will be seen by studying the front elevation that the central span is distinctly broader than the bays on each side of it, in order not to hide or crowd the unusually broad front doorway with its Doric columns in antis and sidelights. This uneven spacing of the columns also gives an hospitable effect to the center entrance, stability to the corners and a delightful rhythm to the whole portico.

length; one facing the main road and the other a side lane. There is a high Doric porch on the street front, reached by a long flight of steps which run parallel with the wall. A delicate diamond design railing is a feature of the porch. There is a wide front doorway with fluted pilasters and double doors of five panels each. The top panels are rounded. On the other façade there is a simple and very flat doorway, not, however, without architectural interest. A pleasing effect of substance and dignity is obtained by the unusually broad treatment of the frame. A moulded architrave of the usual width is separated from the door opening by a plain band seven inches wide and from the narrow clapboards by another plain band, making the total width of the frame eighteen inches. A deep flat arch of solid wood, carved to simulate stone quoins, springs from the outside corners of the frame. The flat arch feature is repeated over all the first floor windows.

The Perkins House, illustrated on page 201, was not built until 1832, but it is surely one of the very best examples of the type of domestic architec-

East Porch
WEBB HOUSE, WINDHAM, CONNECTICUT

PERKINS HOUSE — 1832 — WINDHAM, CONNECTICUT

POMFRET and vicinity: Pomfret owes its origin to the courage of one Captain John Blackwell, an English Puritan, who had fled to America at the restoration of the Stuarts in 1687. He was in Woodstock in its time of peril and panic, caused by the Indian Wars, and rendered valuable service by going out on the "frontier" to what is now Pomfret and "standing his ground" against the enemy.

Mrs. John Grosvenor was among the settlers that straggled into Pomfret after the end of the Indian Wars in 1696. Her portion was the fairest as it did a hundred and fifty years ago. This shallow portico is only six feet wide, with a flat wood ceiling painted lavender blue. The posts are eighteen feet high but only eight inches square at the bottom, tapering to seven inches at the top, giving them a slender, naïve character.

Another two-story portico is found at the Colonel Lyons House at East Woodstock, a few miles north of Pomfret. Four slender and graceful Doric columns support a low pediment roof. A shallow balcony with a picket railing is suspended at the second floor level. The running dia-

BEN GROSVENOR INN, POMFRET, CONNECTICUT

part of the township, the upper part of the present village. Her grandson, Ebenezer Grosvenor, was the noted landlord of the Pomfret Tavern, a resort much frequented in the stirring times just before 1776 when rum and debate flowed with equal freedom.

Prosperous summer residents have modernized and enlarged almost all the simple old eighteenth century houses that once lined Pomfret Street. None are left in their original state except the old Ben Grosvenor Inn, (shown on page 202). Even this has modern additions, but these have been discreetly kept in the rear, so that the long line of the quaint two-story portico still graces the street

mond decoration below the cornice adds to the delicate refinement.

The most surprising and unusual house in the neighborhood is certainly "Squire Bosworth's Castle", at Eastford, (shown on page 203). Built by a wealthy and eccentric bachelor, the house shows much entertaining "individuality" without and within. Perched on a very high, steep hill above the town, the vertical effect is still further enhanced by a two-story monitor roof, containing a lodge room with a fireplace at each end. The interior is literally carved within an inch of its life, with fine scale and highly original motifs worthy of careful inspection.

"SQUIRE BOSWORTH'S CASTLE," EASTFORD, CONNECTICUT

COL. LYONS HOUSE, EAST WOODSTOCK, CONNECTICUT

Detail of Cupola

Detail of Entrance

OLD TOWN HALL, BROOKLYN, CONNECTICUT

BROOKLYN: This pleasant hill town, built around a spacious square green, was not separated from its neighbors Pomfret and Canterbury until 1752. Colonel Godfrey Malbone, a wealthy English loyalist, came here at this time, having escaped from Newport, Rhode Island, where his luxurious home was destroyed by mobs. He soon started to build an Episcopal Church, a copy of Trinity Church, Newport. In the same year the Congregational Meeting House was started in the center of the Green. The two rival churches were completed about the same time. Soon after this came the Revolution, in which Israel Putnam of Brooklyn, won fame for himself and his home town at the Battle of Bunker Hill.

The old white meeting house, with its very tall spire, still stands on the green, with not one graceful detail to relieve its frank austerity. A building more interesting to architects is the old Town Hall near by. One outstanding feature is the entrance doorway, with four Doric pilasters and frieze. The other feature is the square cupola on the roof ridge, with its curved roof, quaint finial and bracketed cornices.

Detail of Palladian Window
SNOW HOUSE, CHAPLIN, CONNECTICUT

CHAPLIN is the latest of the old towns to be founded, but by no means the least interesting. Its first permanent settler was Deacon Benjamin Chaplin, who, in 1740, went from Pomfret out into the "wilderness"—some ten miles to the southwest—took land on the Natchaug River and cleared himself a homestead. In 1747 he married the Widow Mary Ross and built a large and handsome mansion. It still stands, a monument to his success and known yet as the Old Chaplin House. Deacon Chaplin, a man of marked character, shrewd and farsighted, foresaw the growth of the community that was to bear his name, and bought up much land at low figures, laid out farms, built houses and barns and ruled as the lord of the manor. Just why no church was built at the same time we do not know. Certain it is that Deacon Chaplin was a man of religious convictions, for, with a daughter on a pillion behind him to jump down to open intervening bars and gates, he was accustomed to ride six miles to attend church at South Mansfield. At his death, in

1795, he left a generous fund to found a church near his home "before January 1, 1812." Accordingly, a religious society, called after the Deacon, was founded by the farmers living in the neighborhood. But, due to various delays and disagreements, the church was not actually finished until 1820.

The present town of Chaplin extends along a main street, laid parallel with the river. The church is situated about midway of the street, on a slight rise of ground. Although the church itself is of no great architectural interest or merit, there are at least a dozen neighboring houses, rich in fine detail, that are very good examples of the 1820 period.

On each side of the church are twin houses, very similar to a third, the Hope House, at the north end of the town. All three are the two-chimney houses so frequently found in Windham County, with a pediment having a pitch of 30 degrees, enclosing a decorative fan window. The Hope House, the most interesting of the three

SNOW HOUSE—1822—CHAPLIN, CONNECTICUT

JONATHAN CLARK HOUSE — 1827 — CLARK CORNER (NEAR CHAPLIN), CONNECTICUT

HOPE HOUSE—1808—CHAPLIN, CONNECTICUT

is remarkable for its small size—only thirty-four feet front by twenty-four feet in depth—and for its sophisticated and "finished" Georgian detail. An assured hand designed the two Doric pilasters on each corner with back boards and triglyphs, and its influence is also manifest in the mutuled cornice with conspicuously beaded bed moulding.

The Snow House, having a hipped roof and a two-story central motive, set off by two tall pilasters, is not typically representative of Chaplin tradition, but it is none the less interesting. The recessed porch is unusual and surprisingly pleasing and "convincing." The details of its treatment are worthy of careful study. The detail of the well proportioned Palladian window above it and the finely carved frieze below the main cornice (shown on page 205) are also worthy of scrutiny.

The Jonathan Clark House, at Clark Corner, several miles to the south, belongs architecturally to the Chaplin tradition, (see page 207).

Jonathan Clark was a civil engineer and surveyor for more than fifty years. That his experience in the line of his profession, together with the fact that he was also a master-builder, was of great value to him in laying out and planning his house, is evident. It was built in 1827, almost entirely by himself, and upon it he lavished many and intricate forms of ornamentation. In fact, it outdoes all the Chaplin houses in profusion of fine detail. It has the typical tall Doric pilasters and cornice of the Hope House. But, its unique feature is the high and dominating monitor on top of the hipped roof, crowned with a very rich frieze, cornice and latticed railing, (see detail on page 210). The broad recessed doorway, with double pilasters, is in pleasing harmony with the quiet breadth of the front. The wood picket fence, enclosing the dooryard garden, is especially light and agreeable, the round pickets only one inch in diameter, with iron gates to match the pattern of the wood, but even lighter in scale.

"PENNY" LINCOLN HOUSE — 1835 — SCOTLAND, CONNECTICUT

There are other eighteenth century farmhouses in Windham County, scattered sparsely beyond the village greens. They are plainer and perhaps less interesting architecturally than the more prosperous and decorated houses in the towns. There is, however, a definite type found in this county that is exemplified by the "Penny" Lincoln House at Scotland, illustrated above. This two-chimney type is as characteristic of northeastern Connecticut as the one-central-chimney type is typical of central and western Connecticut. The plan consists of four rooms (each about 12 ft. x 18 ft.), two on each side of a central hall, and separated by the large chimneys and deep flanking closets. One of the outer closets is often used as a vestibule to the side door. There

are overhanging gable ends, but no overhangs elsewhere. There are five windows across the fronts, which are approximately forty feet in length, but only two windows across the ends which are approximately thirty feet deep, giving a pleasing contrast of much glass in front and much clapboarding at the ends. Altogether, this type is a stirring example of taste and good proportions, unadorned and needing no adornment.

Whether one prefers the simpler or the more decorated type of house, or one is more sympathetic to the eighteenth century or early nineteenth century type, there are many examples throughout this corner county of Connecticut which remain unspoiled and which are of real architectural interest and appeal.

Detail of Monitor
JONATHAN CLARK HOUSE — 1827 — CLARK CORNER, CONNECTICUT

Old Canterbury on
the Quinnebaug

Text by
Richard H. Dana, Jr.
Photographs by
Kenneth Clark
Originally published in 1923 as White Pine Monograph
Volume IX, Number 6

FIRST CONGREGATIONAL CHURCH, ON THE GREEN, CANTERBURY, CONNECTICUT
Rebuilt in 1784, on the site of former churches.

OLD CANTERBURY ON THE QUINNEBAUG

AMONG the score of early colonial hill towns in Windham County, Connecticut, Canterbury is probably the most interesting and appealing. Not only are there several buildings of unusual architectural merit, but, fortunately these have been preserved in their original state and unspoiled by "modern improvements." In addition to this, the whole village is harmonious, having happily escaped the march of progress and lying peacefully "off the map."

Located on a long irregular ridge, about 200 feet above the broad valley of the Quinnebaug River, this small village has only a dozen old houses near the Green, and another dozen scattered along the old "ways" leading north and south. The result is a town of remarkably intimate and alluring quality.

The calm is unbroken by railroad, trolley or jitney line. Neither does any state road nor motor "tour" pass through the town, with their consequent hot dog stands, gasoline stations and giant billboards. There are no mills, millionaires or summer boarders to bring in money and inevitable changes. There is now but one small general store, and even the former Post Office has been removed to the railroad station, some four miles away. To visit this little town today is therefore quite like stepping back one hundred years or more.

The township of Canterbury was the fourth settlement in the county. The Quinnebaug valley was first settled as early as 1680 by men from Norwich. Major Fitch and his family built the first permanent house in 1697, at what was then called Peagscomsuck, the Indian name for what was later Canterbury. With hundreds of farms and thousands of acres at his disposal, Major Fitch selected for his permanent residence this land near the Quinnebaug River now the township of Canterbury, surely a great compliment from one of his traveled experience.

The town of Plainfield about three miles to the east was organized in 1699. The difficulty, however, of crossing the Quinnebaug River to attend religious worship was the chief ground for starting a separate town organization for Canterbury on the west bank of the river. In 1703, town privileges were granted, and it was formally separated from Plainfield. There were only ten residents, but their "character and circumstances made amends for their small number." They were men of means and position, accustomed to the management of public affairs and well fitted to initiate and carry on the settlement of the new township. But as all of the good land was held by these original ten settlers, there was no inducement for others to join, and the population increased but slowly.

NOTE—Quotes from *History of Windham County*—
by E.D. Larned, 1874.

They soon procured a minister, Rev. Samuel Estabrook, and prepared to build their first Meeting House on the site of the Green. This church was established in 1711 with a membership of only twenty-five.

"Suitable ways" were laid out, connecting the

bridges as the severe ice flows in the early spring kept carrying them away.

Obadiah Johnson was allowed to keep a house for public entertainment "provided he keeps good order," and here town meetings were held and public business transacted. A schoolmaster

Detail of Main Doorway
FIRST CONGREGATIONAL CHURCH, ON THE GREEN, CANTERBURY, CONNECTICUT

town with Plainfield three miles east; Norwich, fifteen miles south; Windham, ten miles west and Woodstock, twenty miles north. These were the closest and only other settlements at this time. The chief difficulty, however, was in maintaining a bridge over the turbulent Quinnebaug. The two towns of Canterbury and Plainfield were put to constant trouble and expense in rebuilding the

was employed to "perambulate" the town, there being no schoolhouse at this time.

Major Fitch was the leading citizen and by far the most picturesque figure in the early days. He was a friend of education and endowed Yale College in 1701 with 600 acres of land. He was genial, generous and hospitable, but somewhat "overconvivial" in his habits; so that he was sometimes

West Front
FIRST CONGREGATIONAL CHURCH—1784—ON THE GREEN, CANTERBURY

compelled to make confessions to the Church as well as to the state. His social position drew many people around him. His plantation was recognized as a place of consequence, the first and, for a long time, the only settlement between Norwich and Woodstock. One of the most prominent men in the whole state, his popularity gradually decreased owing to public jealousy excited by his

one of the most genial and hospitable of men, had a new model house with a conservatory that was the wonder of all the county.

Architecturally it was extremely fortunate that the greatest prosperity of the town came at this period of good taste. After the Civil War, the prosperity declined, there being no special business interests to draw in new residents or keep

PRUDENCE CRANDALL HOUSE, ON THE GREEN, CANTERBURY, CONNECTICUT
Originally built by Squire Elisha Payne.

immense land operations.

The period of greatest prosperity in the town came immediately after the Revolutionary War. Master Adam's School established on the Green in 1796 was an immediate success. The young blood of the town were energetic, and business and trade were active. Cultivated "solid" men gave prominence to the town. Few country towns could boast such social attractions. Dr. Harris,

the young people in the town. Altho' the historian of that time laments the fall of the town from "its former high estate," we cannot but rejoice that it is preserved for us to see, just as it was a century and a half ago.

The most striking piece of architecture in the town is certainly the old Congregational Church, rebuilt in 1784 on the site of former churches. It has a most suitable and commanding position at

Detail of Entrance Pavilion
PRUDENCE CRANDALL HOUSE, ON THE GREEN, CANTERBURY, CONNECTICUT

South Front Entrance
DAVID KINNE HOUSE, BLACK HILL, CANTERBURY, CONNECTICUT

Entrance Pavilion, West Front
CAPTAIN JOHN CLARK HOUSE, SOUTH CANTERBURY, CONNECTICUT

South Front
CAPTAIN JOHN CLARK HOUSE, SOUTH CANTERBURY, CONNECTICUT

the top of the sharply sloping village green, surrounded by fine old maple trees. The recessed porch with its four square Doric columns is an unusual and most fitting solution of the entrance careful study. There are two small side doors from this porch for entrance, and one very broad central double doorway for exit and special occasions. The porch also, being completely protected

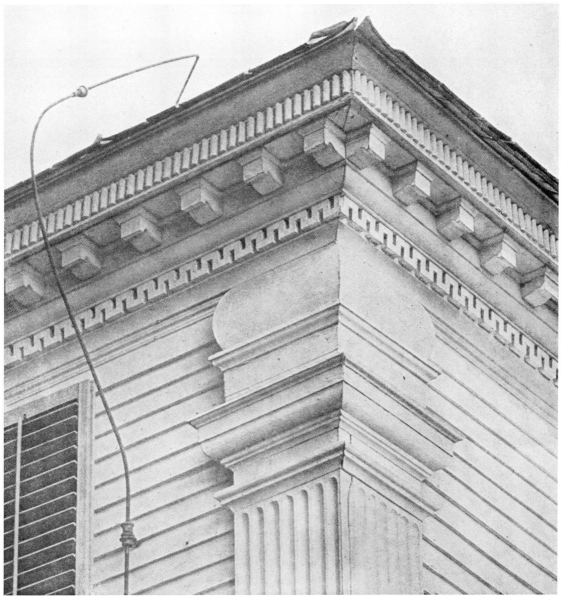

Detail of the Main Cornice
CAPTAIN JOHN CLARK HOUSE, SOUTH CANTERBURY, CONNECTICUT

portico. The recess seems to give it a quiet religious quality not obtained by the usual projecting portico. It seems to invite one to enter in a spirit of quiet and privacy, and is worthy of most on three sides, forms a very sheltered place in bad weather for the congregation to exchange friendly greetings before and after service. The floor is paved with very large granite slabs, and there

West Front

CAPTAIN JOHN CLARK HOUSE, SOUTH CANTERBURY, CONNECTICUT

Built in 1732, enlarged about 1790.

are radiating granite steps outside the center bay. The side bays are protected by a very delicate and inconspicuous picket railing. The octagonal spire is less ornate than many, but entirely pleasing in its proportions. The uneven sides to the octagon and their different treatment are of special interest.

The private houses in the town are generally of quite a distinct type, and were probably all designed by an architect named Dyer. The chief characteristic of this Canterbury type of house is the low-pitched dormerless hip roof, with pediment ends to the deck roof, giving a "semi-monitor" effect. This treatment pleasantly increases the length of the ridge and gives a horizontal footing for the two chimneys. The result gives a comfortable, restful and convincing look to the whole composition.

Another feature of these houses is the two-story pilaster which occurs not only at the corners, but framing the central pavilions on one and often two fronts. Another characteristic is the Palladian window over the front entrance, usually the side windows, as well as the central window having keyed arches. Still another feature is the very wide composition of the front entrance, with pilasters, fanlight and sidelights.

The characteristic most interesting to the architect, however, is the scale and individuality of the conventional late eighteenth century Georgian details. These are usually a little too heavy for domestic purposes and uninteresting in their uniformity. In Canterbury, however, the scale of the details has been slightly reduced with a very just sense of fitness. Examples of the individual variation are seen in the reeding on the cornice and the Greek fret dentil course shown by the detail illustration on page 221, the pilaster caps shown on page 214 and paneled frieze shown on page 218.

The most famous of these old houses is the so-called Prudence Crandall House, originally built by Squire Elisha Payne on the Green. In 1831, Miss Crandall bought the house, left vacant by the Squire's death, and opened a fashionable young ladies' boarding school, much to the pride and satisfaction of the town. About a year later with the support of the leading Abolitionists in Boston, she suddenly changed it to a school for colored girls, much to the disgust and indignation of the aristocratic families. She was threatened with ejection, and even special state legislation against colored schools was put through by her enemies. She was even kept a short while in the Brooklyn jail. But the long drawn out trials brought no definite results, and these persecutions greatly strengthened her friends and supporters. Finally however, all the windows of the house were broken in one night by exasperated townsmen and she and her colored pupils were forced to leave the town. "Thus ended the generous and philanthropic Christian enterprise of Miss Prudence Crandall."

The Crandall house is not a large house. With a frontage of forty-four feet it has a depth of only thirty-two feet. There are four rooms on each floor, separated by two chimneys. The front rooms, however, are about twice as large as the rear rooms. The stair hall goes back only half the depth of the house. The pediment end of the deck roof has an oval decorated with radiating incised lines. The whole oval was formerly painted dark to count as more of a feature than it does at present. The central pavilion facing the Green projects eight inches in the front of the main line of the house, and is typical of the Canterbury type. Fluted pilasters on plain pedestals support the pediment. The second story Palladian window rests on a continuous pedestal—the absolute plainness of which is a pleasing contrast to the surrounding richness.

The next most important house is the Capt. John Clark House at the south end of the town, built about 1732, and enlarged about 1790 by Capt. Clark, an eccentric Englishman with ample means and patriarchal family, who continued his eccentric and autocratic ways until the ripe age of 101. This Clark House is very spacious in every way, with a frontage of forty-six feet and a depth of forty-two feet. The four rooms on each floor are very large and the central hallway running through the entire house is eleven feet wide. The house has two fronts, both treated architecturally. The main front, facing the high road leading to Norwich, has free standing columns, which makes it even more elegant than the Crandall House. The south front, facing the maple lined driveway, has a Roman Doric order enclosing the arched fan, but with no sidelights. Both fronts have very narrow clapboards, only two-and-a-half-inches to the weather, giving an air of great refinement.

The David Kinne House is to the east of the

DAVID KINNE HOUSE, BLACK HILL, CANTERBURY, CONNECTICUT

Built in 1780, enlarged during 1815.

River, on the top of Black Hill, so-called because it was frequently burned over by the Indians. Later, when William Kinne set out a double row of maples along the whole mile of the road leading up to his house, it was suggested that the name be changed to Green Hill. This house was built originally in 1780, with the front facing south. It was enlarged in 1815, the old kitchen at the rear forming a new central hall twelve feet wide opening on to the center of the new east front. It is interesting to note that these two fronts are now identical in treatment. The monitor roof is a direct result of influence from Rhode Island, only a few miles to the east.

Other houses of interest are located on or near the Green. In all there are only a handful. But, like the original citizens of the town, their quality more than makes up for their small number. No unkept lawns, overgrown paths or wandering poultry can in any way lessen their aristocratic assurances. Their sophisticated refinement and good taste are intrinsic and lasting. May they remain unspoiled and cherished for another century at least, a constant joy and inspiration!

Detail of South Entrance
CAPT. JOHN CLARK HOUSE, SOUTH CANTERBURY

Detail of Doorway
LA VALLE HOUSE, CANTERBURY, CONNECTICUT

Detail of Doorway
TURNPIKE HOUSE, CANTERBURY, CONNECTICUT

Old Woodbury, Connecticut

Text by
Wesley S. Bessell
Photographs by
Julian Buckley and The Author
Originally published in 1916 as White Pine Monograph
Volume II, Number 5

Detail of Entrance
SILES HOUSE, LOWER WOODBURY, CONNECTICUT
An example of the two-story motif with pedimented entrance which
was employed in Connecticut in the pre-Revolutionary houses.

OLD WOODBURY AND ADJACENT DOMESTIC ARCHITECTURE OF CONNECTICUT

THE period of our Colonial architecture does not seem very distant when it is viewed in comparison with the history of architecture of the world, and yet in the short three centuries between then and now great changes have taken place to make our modern architecture a conglomerate mass of uninteresting work. Why this unfortunate development should have been permitted to take place when so many examples of the best of our seventeenth and eighteenth century dwellings remain all about us for our guidance and emulation is a source of wonderment to all thinking persons. The rapid growth of the country both in size and wealth may have robbed us of the desire to express ourselves in terms as simple and sweet as those of our forefathers, but why we should have absolutely lost the spirit of the older homes is hard to understand.

Perhaps if we step back to the town of Woodbury in the pleasant little Naugatuck Valley of Connecticut and picture it at the beginning of our Revolutionary struggles we may gain a concise idea of the spirit that then existed but which unfortunately seems to have long since been snuffed out. If we could have been in this quaint town one Sunday morning long ago we could not help but have become imbued with its atmosphere. It was a clear, bright morning, one long to be remembered by the inhabitants. The British at Boston had already marched out and met the minutemen, and now the men and boys of Woodbury expected to depart in order to join Washington's command, and on this particular Sunday, just after service at the North Church, a band of men were to leave their homes, some for long periods, others for all time. As the bell tolled in the belfry of North Church, which Hezikiah Platt had designed and built and whose history was to be written in later times, fate decreed that one Jonathan, son of Hezikiah, was here to take leave of Sally Orton, daughter of William Orton. Outlined above the trees the North Church spire stood, dignified, pure white, and delicate of design. In the play of light and shadow, the pilastered front supporting the pediment in which the green blind spread in fan-like shape blended well with the blue and pale yellow facings of the Continental army uniforms so proudly worn by the boys of Woodbury. Sally and Jonathan were wont to take leave, for they were childhood sweethearts, and the Orton House was soon no longer to have Jonathan Platt swing on the picket gate and call to Sally, and then hide behind the stately rose bush that covered its entrance. Just beyond this scene stood the Orton House with its quaint wooden doorway and rough stone doorstep, which had served to bind these two. Grown to sweet maidenhood, she had opened this same door for him, for his tap on the knocker was as well known to Sally as his laughter, and if in her anxiety to answer that knock she upset the candleholder from its lodging place, we can now forgive her for the charred lace work that suffered for her haste. When once inside the stair hall with its stairway of turned balusters and newels, carved scrolls at the open end of the strings, one could see that it was all the work of the elder Platt. Jonathan was ushered into the parlor. Here he could gaze upon the handiwork of his parent by way of a paneled mantel and wainscot, but his gaze rested not long on his father's labors, but upon a pretty face in a poke bonnet, and strange as it may seem, the work of one Hezikiah Platt was no longer thought of. Hezikiah Platt was responsible in his small way for many of the buildings of Woodbury, for he had built for one Abner Lockwood the house at Long Hill where the

Benjamin had been their architectural guides, and they could not break from the tradition that had been established.

The soldiers from Woodbury left by the post road on this memorable Sunday—left behind all that was theirs, the places their fathers and they had created out of wood and masonry. Shaded streets grew narrow as they passed by the old tavern in the bend of the road where they were lost to view. Over a rise they could still see the North Church spire, quietly nestling in the beautiful valley; and by the church

ORTON HOUSE, WOODBURY, CONNECTICUT

Home of Sally Orton

road turns sharp on its way to Sandy Hook, and the Siles House in lower Woodbury with its pedimented entrance, and then the Judson House, and the Bostwick House, with its simple entrance flanked by well proportioned windows on which the blinds gave a charming color against the white pine clapboards. Yes, the elder Platt had played an important part in the building up of Woodbury, but as things were reckoned then, his houses were but of a type, exemplified by others, similar in design but different in detail, and no one thought but of this kind of house, for had they not all lived the simple life, and why should they not carry out the portrayal of what life was to them in their homes of wood? Beatty Langley and Asher

sat Sally Orton, not daring to raise her head, for her very life had gone forth, and Woodbury's youth and manhood, and particularly Jonathan Platt's, were now facing a duty made necessary by oppression, a duty that meant, if well done, the keeping of home and family together—the homes they had built with their own hands, the homes that they had worked for and in which they had taken so much pride. These must stand, must exist, for they were part of themselves. Had not Absalom Turnbull, the village smith, forged the hinges and moulded the knobs on those houses, was not the timber hewn from the clearing and run through the saw by their hands? And so it was that the work of our forefathers, created in mind and modeled in wood, was now to be protected by such men who, going forth to preserve their handiwork, counted not the cost.

This spirit existed at that time, this spirit still exists, but why has the present generation lapsed into a don't-care feeling regarding what home is or can be made? Why do we who sally forth nowadays, familiar as we are with these works of our forefathers, permit the atrocities committed by the so-much-per-yard mills and ten-dollar-per-house, profit-taking contractors? Home does not mean much

strange to say, this is what he thinks is beautiful. One wonders what Jonathan Platt, going forth to protect, and Sally Orton, remaining in the background to keep in order for his home-coming the old Orton House with its hollyhocks, foxgloves, and boxwood hedge, with its quiet simplicity, would think if they could view these modern so-called homes. One cannot help but wonder also if the man of today has lost the desire for beauty or if it has only been taken away from him by the constant presentation of something hideous. Let us hope that the latter

HOUSE AT WOODBURY, CONNECTICUT
Jonathan Platt's Home

to these concerns. The pride taken in and thought given to his buildings by Hezikiah Platt do not interest them. Their chief thoughts and interest are commercial ones, and the houses which they produce are usually sad and material examples of what not to do. The beautiful villas with special mention of "Colonial" style advertised for sale by our present day get-rich-quick-build-a-house-over-night realty developers are the blight of our architectural development. How one wishes the word "villa" had never existed, and that it might constitute a crime to desecrate the word "colonial."

This is what we see today—this is what the average citizen is buying and building, and,

is the case, and that there are numerous Jonathan Platts and Sally Ortons, and that all that is needed for the betterment of our domestic architecture is the removal of the evil manner in which it is created.

Jonathan returns to Woodbury after having served his country well, and Sally is there to greet him. Of course the boxwood hedge is larger, and the rose bush almost hides from view the gate, but all is the same upon his return as far as the house is concerned. The descendants of Jonathan and Sally, taking up where they left off, continued the work of their fathers, for did not the Dennings and Captain Asubel Arnold build according to tradition? Their houses on the bend of the road are pure

Colonial. And until the Greek Revival there was no departure from a general type; even with the advent of the Neo-Grec it was so woven into these older creations that no real damage was done, but after this period chaos ran rampant, and as a result we find the nondescripts which unfortunately are with us today, the so-called Elizabethan, Gothic and Queen Anne houses with their paper doily edging and verge board scalloping in imitation of pantry shelving paper.

Unfortunately this period acted like a blight on America's architecture, for it fastened itself to the pure examples which fell into its hands, and today it is difficult to find a

Detail of Corner Board
JABES BACON HOUSE, WOODBURY

In this example a bead takes the place of a stile between the panels. The panel mould miters with the lowest member of the overhang mouldings.

house, either old or new, which is free from its ravages.

It is with a great deal of inward satisfaction and pleasure, however, that we note that the descendants of Jonathan and Sally are again rising to meet and prevent such conditions from going on unchecked. Today there is a refreshing influence at work in our midst for the construction of houses for these descendants. A new Jonathan Platt and Sally are taking up the work where the former left off. Our architecture is assuming a definite character, and surely will be benefited by the careful study being made by this new generation of architects, who are delving into the beauties of

JABES BACON HOUSE, ON THE LOWER ROAD, WOODBURY, CONNECTICUT
One of the earliest Woodbury houses of the double overhang type. The clapboards are fastened by boat nails left clearly exposed and painted over. The porch is of much later date.

LOCKWOOD HOUSE, CROMWELL, CONNECTICUT

The main house is over two hundred years old. The gambrel-
roofed ell composes nicely with the single-pitch roof of the house.

HOUSE NEAR SANDY HOOK, CONNECTICUT, ON THE SOUTHBURY ROAD

Typical of the early eighteenth-century houses of the lean-to variety in this section.
The window are divided into twenty-four lights. The original gutters were of wood.

HOUSE ON THE LOWER ROAD, WOODBURY, CONNECTICUT

A most picturesque composition nestling in valley. One of the few homes remaining in almost their original state; the unsightly modern leader across the end is unfortunate.

OLD GLEBE HOUSE—1771—LOWER ROAD, WOODBURY, CONNECTICUT

The very broad corner boards are paneled on both sides without using a stile and the moulding is returned across the top. The first Episcopalian bishop in America was selected in this house.

Door blinds add much charm and color to this example. There is something of quaintness and homeliness about these simple blinds.

Rather a good entablature. The triglyphs are not logical in the frieze of a porch of this kind, but are often found, however, in Colonial examples.

TWO PORCHES IN OLD WOODBURY, CONNECTICUT

the older examples, obtaining in their work those qualities and that spirit of quaintness known as America's gifts to the architecture of the world, which have been so long neglected by those responsible for our domestic architecture. This Colonial architecture of our forefathers is again about to come into its own; indeed, there are today many instances where we may discover work which is faithful in every way to the best of our early traditions. There is a reversion to a consideration of those subtle qualities which produced the many homes of past centuries that possess a charm that age alone cannot give, but which is the result of that true art of the Colonial builders whose lives were expressed in the design of their dwellings. It is to be hoped that this interest which is being manifested in the best of the old examples of housebuilding will prevent any further spread of past building evils. That these evils can be removed is certain, but it needs the sincere and untiring help of every one, both in the profession and out. Cosmopolitan America can and should develop a type, and that type may readily have the Colonial traditions as a basic principle.

SANFORD HOUSE, LITCHFIELD, CONNECTICUT

OLD SLAVE QUARTERS OF THE BACON HOUSE, WOODBURY, CONNECTICUT
This building is now used as a tea house.

OLD HOUSE AT RIDGEFIELD, CONNECTICUT
The lines of the porch roof have been softened by a very happy treatment.

MARSHALL HOUSE, WOODBURY, CONNECTICUT

The wing is the original house and is over two hundred and thirty years old. The row of two-story columns of the living-porch is characteristic of this section and a pleasing method of handling the piazza problem.

BOSTWICK HOUSE, SOUTHBURY, CONNECTICUT

The fenestration is excellent for a small house and the detail of cornice and window trim very carefully designed.

Detail of Entrance Porch
BOSTWICK HOUSE, SOUTHBURY, CONNECTICUT
A good example of this type of porch with wood-paneled soffit of the hood. The seats at the side are modern.

Connecticut Valley Houses

Text by
Richard B. Derby
Photographs by
Julian Buckley
Originally published in 1916 as White Pine Monograph
Volume II, Number 3

Detail of Entrance Doorway
COLTON HOUSE, LONGMEADOW, MASSACHUSETTS

EARLY HOUSES OF THE CONNECTICUT VALLEY

THE Connecticut Valley was first settled by exiles from Massachusetts in 1636. The original settlements in Springfield and other communities in Massachusetts and also in the so-called River Towns of Connecticut, Hartford, Windsor and Wethersfield, broke up from time to time, and the seceders formed new settlements along the river valley at other points. At the same time the first settled towns were augmented by the arrival of new members from the coast. Within a comparatively short time territory was intermittently occupied between, say, Northampton and Wethersfield, over a distance of one hundred miles or so. Their first dwellings were merely cellars, which, however, speedily gave place to a kind of house which became typical of the so-called first period work. The plan of these houses was little more than two rooms on either side of the chimney, in front of which was the stair leading out of the hall into which the front door opened. The second story was the same as the first, although in some cases the rooms were slightly larger by reason of an overhang. This early plan was altered by the addition of a shed on the rear, making the typical plan of the second period, and this again was altered to make the third period by raising the addition a full two stories, and by the consequent change in roofing to the gambrel.

Thence we have shift to the two end chimneys, altering their positions and occupying such a place with regard to the rooms that the resultant plan resembles two of the earlier plans put side by side, with a hallway running between them. These types overlapped each other in various ways, but eventually gave place as essential types to the Greek influence, which began to be felt, perhaps, around 1800.

The Connecticut Valley work had some few characteristics of its own, due to local material or the importation direct from England of craftsmen working in slightly differing methods. The chimneys, for instance, were largely built of stone, since stone was plentiful and brick, of course, was not. The brick ovens which we find inserted in the chimneys were not, as a rule, contemporary with them. The summer beams ran from chimney to end wall, as in the houses of the Plymouth Colony, instead of parallel with the chimney girt, as in the early houses of other communities. The use under the overhang of both drop and bracket is a Connecticut characteristic, as are also the brackets under the gable, though the use of brackets under the verge board is not uncommon elsewhere. Perhaps the most striking characteristic of this Connecticut Valley work in the matter of design is to be found in the entrance treatment of the houses. The doors themselves were double doors, paneled in a manner not elsewhere to be found. One writer refers the paneling to Jacobean precedent. The frames around these also were markedly distinctive. Three types stand out, all of which are broad, of course, by reason of the wide door openings: the frames which have the flat entablatures, those with simple pediments, and those with broken pediment frames, which are perhaps more typical than the others. On the detail of all of these, particularly the latter, much careful workmanship is lavished. It varies from a kind which follows precedent to that which is unique, much of the latter being pure inspiration on the owner's or builder's part. It would seem as if the builders of the earlier houses found much entertainment in exercising their ingenuity upon the detail of their entrances, without, however, departing from their general type.

WHITMAN HOUSE, FARMINGTON, CONNECTICUT
Noteworthy as an example of the overhang construction with original drops and stone chimney.

WILLIAMS HOUSE, EAST HARTFORD, CONNECTICUT
Characteristic of Connecticut third period work.

Man loves any material that he has worked upon in proportion to its resistance to his efforts of bending it to his will—assuming that he has not attempted the impossible or the absurd with reference to the task at hand. This is why the hand-hewn timber of our old houses is better than the two by four sawed stud or the six by eight post. I can very well believe that the first settlers in Connecticut took their timbers for their houses with them, as they are said to have done. They had wrought upon them with their own hands, and had a certain affection for them on this account, and what is equally important, the timbers had an affection for the men who had worked them. The frames of our present houses are a pretty good example of efficiency in the economic and modern sense. Its loads have been carefully appraised and distributed proportionately over the members which it supports, so that the strain and stress on each of these is just precisely what each one will bear, and never more or less. This may be all right, as no doubt it is from the scientific or the economic point of view, but it represents for me a very low order of efficiency.

I look at the ten by twelve corner posts in the summer kitchen of my great-grandfather's old home, and I wonder whether he knew that four by six posts would have done the work of these. Perhaps he did, and perhaps he did not, and perhaps he did not care whether it would have done the work or not; but I feel sure that he would never have had the satisfaction out of our smaller post that he must have experienced from the ten by twelve. My great-grandfather had the reputation in his district of being able to square the butt of a log more perfectly than any one else around, and he left a better stump in his wood lot than his neighbors did. I am sure, therefore, that he applied himself with great care to the corner posts, beams and rafters of his own home, that he had a defensible pride in the result of his handiwork, and that he never could have had this pride in any four by six. The affection which he had for his timbers was returned by them, and is being returned today. I get back some of it always when I look at the smoky corner posts, or when I lie on the bed in the unfinished attic and let my eyes wander over the hand-hewn rafters.

Connecticut settlers of 1636 forged their way westward from Massachusetts through uncharted forests. They cut their own paths, except, perhaps, for short distances, where they found an Indian trail making in their direction. Besides their axes they must have carried arms; for, though the Indians were politically friendly, they were hardly to be trusted in every case.

They must have carried, too, some provisions and their camping outfits, for they did not know that they would always have luck in finding food, and they were quite uncertain in what places or at what times they would pitch their tents. It is hardly to be believed, therefore, that they carried timber along with the other things on their backs, or that they added this to the burdens of their horses. It is not incredible, however, that, the Connecticut Valley once reached, they had their timbers brought in the vessels which made the first long voyage around the cape and up the river to the place of their abode. They were engaged primarily in clearing and planting, and, no doubt, their energies were fully occupied with these exertions.

The first houses, as we know, were merely cellars dug in the side of a hill, the walls lined with stone or logs; the roofs simply lean-tos brushed or thatched. These crude shelters gave place to better habitations in comparatively short time. The very early dwellings were likely built of white pine, and in certain instances of oak, squared and bored and ready to be raised and pinned together.

Fetching timber from Massachusetts could hardly have continued long. It was too much like bringing coals to Newcastle. The timber was abundant, and the craftsmen instinct must have cried aloud to exercise itself.

We are not acquainted with the aspect of the forest which these settlers looked out upon, and we do not know precisely the feelings which the native trees engendered under the conditions which obtained; but some of us are not so young but that we have seen native forests, and the impression these have made upon us (though of a later time and under widely changed conditions) is not perhaps so very different from that made on the earliest inhabitants of Western Massachusetts and Connecticut. I myself remember very well the primeval forests of the Alleghany Mountains in Pennsylvania. I remember when I first rode over them on a tote-team, and later tramped my way, with pack on back, beneath the pine and hemlock. The lowest branches of these trees were far above me. I should hardly dare to guess how far, but I can recollect distinctly that the rhododendrons which flourished in the dusk below them interlaced their lowest branches several times my height above my head, and the blossoms of the topmost branches must have been thirty or more feet in height. The butts of the trees themselves were huge, and the whole effect or feeling (one does not observe the forest) for me was the same that I get from looking at a lofty mountain. I do not wish to try to match my strength against a mountain, and I did not (as I now remember) wish to build myself a cabin of these trees.

This was not the feeling, however, of the men who worked among them. These trees, or the making of them into timber, was their life. They were not depressed but rather tempted and exhilarated by the size and number of them; it was their pride, like my great-grandfather's, to square a butt with axes or to notch one so exactly that the tree would fall precisely where they meant it should. They saw only the tree that could be felled and subdivided, barked and piled on skidways and later take its booming way for miles along the frosty slide to

water, whence it could be splashed or floated to the sawmills. These lumbermen had both strength and genius for this work, and no doubt the earlier settlers had it also. In addition, they had an instinct for building their homes.

The earliest houses which they built have not come down to us. The Indians, who were friendly for the first years, took the war-path, and the life of the settlers for perhaps a hundred years included a constant warfare for defense among its other duties. As the whites increased in number they were more able to protect themselves. The first settlements were frequently destroyed. Springfield was burned in 1675 and Deerfield met the same fate twice, —smaller places even more frequently. Men,

WAIT HOUSE, SOUTH LYME, MASSACHUSETTS
Unsymmetrical placing of the windows.

OLD HOUSE AT FARMINGTON, CONNECTICUT
Gambrel of the third period with plan of the first period.

women and children were butchered by scores and many were carried into captivity. One writer* has said: "There is hardly a square acre and certainly not a square mile of the Connecticut Valley that has not been tracked by the flying feet of fear, resounded with the groan of the dying, drunk the blood of the dead or served as the scene of toils made doubly toilsome by an apprehension of danger that never slept." In spite of this the towns grew slowly, for the inhabitants—such of them as were left—came back and rebuilt their homes.

Most of these houses we find were doubtless built not earlier than 1650, and I myself feel reasonably sure only of work as many as ten years later. This, of course, was modeled

THOMAS LEE HOUSE, EAST LYME, MASSACHUSETTS
Original part of house built about 1660.

from the earliest type of house and has the hand-hewn timbers put together according to the logic and efficiency of this early time. The examples of the first period are to be found mostly in Connecticut, and even here in the southern part of the valley. After these, as we go north, we find examples of the two succeeding periods, and in the northern part of the Connecticut Valley we find examples of the Greek influence. This does not mean that the late work is found, but rather that the earlier work is not found (or at least that I have not found it) in the northern part. Here in the valley, as elsewhere in the country, we find the earlier builders the craftsmen of their own

*Holland, *History of Western Massachusetts.*

DEMING HOUSE, WETHERSFIELD, CONNECTICUT
Center doorway with one window on either side.

FRAME WITH SIMPLE PEDIMENT

FRAME WITH FLAT ENTABLATURE

TWO OF THE TYPES OF CONNECTICUT VALLEY DOORWAYS

Literal copies in wood of Georgian stone doorways made before Colonial woodworkers had learned the more graceful and more delicate possibilities of wood as a building material, yet early enough to show still a trace of Gothic feeling in the lower panels.

Entrance Porch
HOUSE AT GLASTONBURY, CONNECTICUT
Much of the charm of this porch may be the charm of age, but it is finely proportioned and of refined detail.

Detail of Entrance
WILLIAMS HOUSE, DEERFIELD, MASSACHUSETTS
A doorway with broken pediment which claims to have been built in 1750, the same year as the house, but is probably several decades later.

WHEELER HOUSE, ORFORD, NEW HAMPSHIRE

It is believed this house was done by Bulfinch.

houses, and here as elsewhere we find the crafts-men limited to the work of the building craft. In proportion as time advanced and the settlements increased in size, people pursued more and more strictly their own business, and more and more called in outsiders, who were builders only, to construct their houses for them. This meant that the builders, in fulfilling all their obligations, economized their time by milling their logs instead of squaring them by hand. They used nails instead of wooden pins and used manufactured nails instead of hand-wrought ones. In this way they got more and more out of touch with the materials in which and with which they worked, and so, of course, they had less affection for them. The good old beams were first cased and then entirely concealed behind plaster, being reduced in size to meet merely structural needs. Interest became cen-

tered in the things that were apparent outside as well as inside the house, and this tendency continued until we today are giving our interest and attention to the detail which superficially appears.

It would be interesting to do an old house as the old men would have done it, and it is likely that most architects would welcome a chance to do this if it offered. Big white pine timber grows abundantly today, though no longer in the East and at our very doors, but the facilities of transportation may almost do away with the handicap of this condition. Let some big lumberman offer us his large timbers and see whether this may not result in a reversion in some degree to older architectural types. These types, when added to our present ones, would furnish a broader basis of tradition on which to build our future native work.

ELLSWORTH HOUSE, WINDSOR, CONNECTICUT
Two-story end treatment is interesting. Classic proportions for columns have
been disregarded, resulting in a delicacy which is peculiarly appropriate to wood.

HOUSE AT HILLSTEAD, FARMINGTON, CONNECTICUT

Excellent but rather sophisticated example of type of house which embraces
elements of design from several periods, all probably earlier than itself.

HOUSE OF GOVERNOR RICHARD GRISWOLD — 1800 — BLACKHALL, CONNECTICUT

An unusual and interesting composition in spite of the regrettable bay.

HORATIO HOYT HOUSE, DEERFIELD, MASSACHUSETTS

Excellent example of Connecticut Valley variety of a type of house common to New England.

FRARY HOUSE, DEERFIELD, MASSACHUSETTS

North portion built in 1683. An L variety of the above Hoyt type of house.

Detail of Side Entrance Doorway
FRARY HOUSE, DEERFIELD, MASSACHUSETTS
Excellent in proportion and in well-executed detail.

DETAIL·OF·CORNER·

SCALE·FOR·DETAILS

·FRONT·E

·FIRST·FI

THE·BRI

·ANNAPOLIS